A Way with Words

Preaching That Transforms Congregations

Adam T. Trambley

CHURCH
PUBLISHING
INCORPORATED

Church Publishing
19 East 34th Street
New York, NY 10016
www.churchpublishing.org

Cover design by Jennifer Kopec, 2Pug Design
Typeset by Perfectype, Nashville, Tennessee

Library of Congress Cataloging-in-Publication Data

Names: Trambley, Adam T., author.
Title: A way with words : preaching that transforms congregations / Adam T.
   Trambley.
Identifiers: LCCN 2019052347 (print) | LCCN 2019052348 (ebook) | ISBN
   9781640652545 (paperback) | ISBN 9781640652552 (ebook)
Subjects: LCSH: Preaching.
Classification: LCC BV4211.3 .T725 2020 (print) | LCC BV4211.3 (ebook) |
   DDC 251--dc23
LC record available at https://lccn.loc.gov/2019052347
LC ebook record available at https://lccn.loc.gov/2019052348

A Way
with
Words

For Jane

With gratitude to all those who have helped me become a better preacher, especially Jane, Lily, and Julia, the congregations at St. John's in Sharon, Trinity Memorial in Warren, and the Church of St. Clement in Alexandria, Sean Rowe, Bob Logan, Ben Campbell, Dave Daubert, Robert Edeburn, David Frazelle, Abbey Alter, Jill Niess, Ruthanna Hooke, Judith McDaniel, Eric Williams, Dan Martins, John Hortum, and the preachers at the Paulist Center in Boston.

Contents

Foreword

THE LEAST EFFECTIVE sermon in history is recounted for us in the book of Exodus. It was such a spectacular failure that it has become one of the foundational stories of our faith.

You know how it goes. In Exodus 20, God delivers the Ten Commandments to Moses. The people are willing to hear about these new laws, but not directly from God. "You speak to us, and we will listen," they say to Moses, "but do not let God speak to us, or we will die."

So Moses addresses the people and delivers the commandments. The very first one is simple: "You shall have no other gods before me." After he is done preaching, Moses goes back up Mt. Sinai to get some more laws and instructions for building a tabernacle. Predictably, he isn't gone long before the Israelites decide to melt down some gold and make another god.

The scriptures tell us that in the aftermath of this homiletical failure, about three thousand people died and those who survived were struck with a plague. This is worth remembering when you preach a sermon that doesn't go the way you had hoped. No matter what, it will not go as badly for you as it did for Moses.

In this volume, Adam Trambley provides what we need to succeed precisely where Moses failed. With practical guidance and real-life examples, Adam helps us consider how our sermons—especially sermon series that unfold over weeks or months—can help the people of God see new visions and grasp new possibilities.

Adam's advice is timely. In many ways, those of us who preach in the mainline church are in a wilderness time. The institutions we lead are facing what organizational development scholars call adaptive challenges, meaning that they cannot be solved by the expertise and skills that we currently have. The only way to address these challenges—like the church's contracting human and financial resources, inequality and division in the world around us, and dramatic cultural shifts in the ways people find spiritual meaning—is to wander for a time.

Preaching in the wilderness, as Moses learned, is harder than it looks. But when our familiar signposts have disappeared, focused engagement with scripture in the form of weekly sermons can help the people of God find vision and exercise creativity. Bold and effective preaching can help us travel out of the wilderness to the promised land of freedom and new life in Christ.

The pages that follow can serve as a travel guide to those of us called to preach in these uncertain times. Adam is no armchair traveler; for more than a decade, he has served as rector of St. John's Episcopal Church in Sharon, Pennsylvania, a town situated on the border of Pennsylvania and Ohio in the heart of the depopulating Rust Belt. In Sharon, Adam and the people he leads have fostered growth in spirituality and stewardship while building long-term ministries that serve a community where more than a quarter of children live below the poverty line. Adam's preaching series, as you will read, have been a linchpin of the congregation's vitality.

In the book's second part, you will find practical, real-world tips about strengthening your preaching with prayer, physical exercises, and a clear and authentic understanding of your vision of the kingdom of God and what the apostle Peter calls "the hope that is in you." Adam delivers this advice, amassed over a preaching career of more than two decades, with candid stories of his own development as a preacher and anecdotes that will help even the most wizened preachers up their game.

As we journey in the wilderness of the twenty-first century, the scriptures invite us to imagine anew the ways we are called to participate in God's mission. When we bring those stories alive through our preaching, as Adam shows us how to do, our churches can be transformed for the sake of the gospel, and the story of God's saving deeds in history becomes ours.

The Rt. Rev. Sean W. Rowe
Bishop of Northwestern Pennsylvania and Western New York
Consecration of Samuel Seabury 2019

Introduction

IN SEMINARY, we were taught that the congregation should clearly know the main point we were trying to make. After every sermon preached in class, our professor went to the board and asked, "What did you hear?" Sometimes what the preacher thought the sermon said matched what was heard, but usually, especially at the beginning of the semester, the gap between intent and impact was pretty large.

Exercises like this are essential in helping new preachers learn the art of getting their message across. Even the most experienced preachers can sometimes be amazed by what parishioners tell them about their sermons in the receiving line after service. We all need to be proficient in the art of sermon preparation and delivery. Faithful exegesis and competent rhetorical techniques matter greatly to preachers and their listeners.

Unfortunately, the basic homiletical skills I encountered in seminary or read about in preaching books were not adequate to deal with the reality I faced in my parishes. Sitting in the pews were people who had been in church much of their lives and had a clear sense of what they thought their faith and their congregational life should be. Any "point" I made in a single sermon, however clearly expounded, wasn't going to alter those expectations. The congregation might learn something new, and some of them might even embark on my important suggestion of the week, but the rubber band of their faith life snapped back quickly. Even more troubling to me, their current understanding of their faith and their congregational life was not leading to a thriving, growing church.

In this context, preaching became vitally important. Where else could I share a message of the reign of God that might move people? Yet, the overarching goal of my preaching had to develop. Instead of choosing one main point each Sunday and working to deliver it effectively, I began to look for a way to think about my preaching that would help me accomplish the larger adaptive task before me. A breakthrough came when I began to think of myself as preaching one continuous sermon over a course of eighteen months, rather than a series of different sermons week after week.

This book is designed to help a preacher think about preaching a sermon that lasts between one and three years. While the topics covered could be applied in almost any preaching context, some situations can most benefit from these concepts. First, I assume that you and your congregation connect frequently. You are the primary preacher and a large portion of the congregation is there more weeks than not. Second, I also assume that your connections are not just in the pulpit, but that you are the primary pastoral caregiver and the leader of the church board. Third, I assume that your congregation needs to make some significant changes to grow and thrive. These changes could be helping a sleepy congregation start evangelizing, directing the congregation to meet a new neighborhood challenge, or convincing a growing congregation to focus on developing the structures needed for the next stages of development. In the rapidly changing environment we live in, every congregation needs to make some significant changes to be who God is calling them to be in the next phase of their life.

However you read this book, I hope that you will have a new perspective on how to approach preaching from a long-term perspective, while being challenged to preach with greater prayer, passion, personality, and physicality. God's call to us as preachers and as leaders of congregations is too important to take one sermon at a time or to give anything less than our full selves.

— Part 1 —

The Long-Term Sermon

– 1 –

Teaching a New Language

You were taught to put away your former way of life . . .
and to be renewed in the spirit of your minds, and to
clothe yourselves with the new self, created according to
the likeness of God in true righteousness and holiness.

—Ephesians 4:22–24

PAUL'S WORDS EXPRESS the challenge for pastors. We strive to teach God's people to put away their former understandings and practices in favor of new life created in the righteousness and holiness of God. Then, when we look out at the congregation as we prepare to preach, we don't see what we hoped. Most every Sunday morning we have offered the congregation what (we think) they needed to know in three rhetorically balanced and clearly expressed points. Heads nodded, notes were taken, and, perhaps, even an occasional "Amen" was muttered. Yet the evidence of our words taking root, much less bearing fruit, can be lacking in the parish's life and ministry. Paul dealt with that situation by writing a six-chapter letter, but that approach is unlikely to be as successful in our contemporary congregational lives. We need another way to think about

3

what we are trying to accomplish in our preaching, and how we evaluate our success.

Our goals and evaluation are more difficult in congregations that have been around for a while. A congregation with dozens of new Christians showing up each month might look at baptisms or new members with some satisfaction. Most of us preach in a different context, however. The majority of churches, especially in the United States, are smaller and have a slower trickle of new members. While the eventual goal of preaching may be to get our wider community to come into personal relationship with Jesus Christ, our more immediate work with the people of God needs to have intermediate goals. The preaching task in these situations is to help the faithful in our community to make the needed changes in their individual and parish lives so they can live out the Great Commission and the Great Commandment.

The world outside of the red church doors is not the same world most of our current church members were brought up in. We all know that. Changes in travel and communication, changes in extended family relationships and commitments, and changes in work and school activity schedules have all turned the traditional role of the local church upside down. Add to these practical changes the spiritual challenges of generations who are unfamiliar with the basic Christian narrative and an increase in a variety of non-Christian spiritualities, and the preacher has an enormous task to help even the most dedicated congregation respond effectively to the world around them.

Regardless of the big societal changes around us, we know that important, smaller-scale changes also need to happen regularly in a congregation's life. After years of focusing on an outreach program, we may need to do more evangelism. When the largest Sunday school class in recent years graduates, the teachers may need a break to go to a Bible study class themselves. We may need, for painfully obvious reasons, to drop everything and work on conflict resolution and rebuilding loving relationships. The changes and transitions that seem most straightforward to us still require time and patience to lead a congregation through them.

I remember getting frustrated by what seemed to me to be the glacially slow pace of the congregation coming to understand the need for an obvious change. Then I realized my time and the congregation's time did not progress at the same pace. I was focusing on the parish's life, conservatively, forty to fifty hours each week. For a particularly important issue like the one I was dealing with, some part of my brain was probably concerned about it almost every waking moment. (I know that isn't healthy, but most of us have been there about some issue or another.) Unfortunately, from my perspective, no one else in the parish was quite that consumed. My core leaders spent maybe five to ten hours a week focusing on the parish, which was very faithful. The issues I processed in one week took my leaders five to ten weeks. Most of these same leaders, however, had also been in the church for a long time. They had spent decades at church, learning one way of operating and diligently living that way out. When I preached, or spoke to them outside of the pulpit, I wasn't starting from a blank slate. Tapes were already playing in their brains—tapes that had to be erased and rewritten. No wonder things took so long, even for the church's dedicated leadership. For the person in the pew, who may average two hours of church time each week for two or three Sundays a month, things take even longer. A change that took me an intense week to process may take more than a year for the bulk of the congregation to understand and live into.

People who study change know how long the process takes. They also understand how frustrated leaders can get, and so warn against impatience. In his book *Leading Change,* John Kotter says that one of the primary reasons that change efforts fail is that the vision for change is undercommunicated by at least a factor of ten and maybe a factor of a hundred or a thousand.[1] I know that when something is important enough for the congregation for me to spend two or three sermons on it, by the time I've finished I feel like I have said everything I need to

---

1. John Kotter, *Leading Change* (Boston, MA: Harvard Business School Press, 1996), 9.

say; I'm ready to move on. Kotter cautions me, however, that maybe the congregation still needs to hear it another twenty or thirty times. Or maybe even another two hundred or two thousand times. When I think about important changes that did not take root in the way that I had hoped, I can usually find places where I stopped sharing the vision for that particular change far too soon. Maybe a crisis came up, maybe I began a push right before Holy Week or the summer or another time that pulled away everyone's energy and attention, or maybe I just got bored and moved on.

Change, of course, doesn't happen in a clean, linear kind of way. The reign of God doesn't materialize simply because we gave twenty sermons or even two thousand sermons instead of two. Even so, thinking about the time spent does tell us something about how we might approach our effectiveness as leaders who preach. One piece of good news from Kotter is that many of the same elements that make up good preaching are also the best ways to help people understand the vision for change. Kotter lists as key communication elements the techniques of drawing verbal pictures, repetition, leadership by example, explaining perceived inconsistencies, and elimination of "jargon and technobabble."[2] His two other elements are communications basics that we can easily incorporate if we think about preaching more expansively than the fifteen minutes following the gospel reading. Kotter suggests using multiple forums and having opportunities for give-and-take.[3] Many preachers have found their sermons more effective by getting feedback afterwards or even input before preaching, and every congregation has multiple avenues available for a pastor to reinforce their vision.

We know, too, that good preaching is going to illuminate and reinforce the work being done in the rest of the congregation's life. Today, perhaps more than any time in the last century, the sermon is foundational in leading a congregation to where God is calling. No longer can a

---

2. Kotter, *Leading Change*, 90.
3. Kotter, *Leading Change*, 90.

quality sermon expect to see fruit by merely instructing, cheerleading, or exhorting. If the sermon's purpose is to get people to do one thing or to make one change, we are probably thinking too small. The person who pays close attention and does whatever is asked might go home and try a spiritual exercise, read a Bible passage, or find a way to bring up Jesus in one conversation that week. Then, the following week, they will drop that discipline in favor of a newly assigned sermon task. Such behaviors aren't the fruit we need. Instead, we need to preach a new approach and understanding, with corresponding new actions and habits, and such preaching takes significant time and intentionality.

I believe that our contemporary preaching task is more like teaching people a new language than it is getting them to do something at the end of the sermon. When children are learning a language, the act of speaking and reading allows them to gain the skills, experience, and worldview needed to be able to process what they need to hear. This approach does not make any of the individual books or conversations unimportant. On the contrary, each particular element becomes even more important because not only does the content need to be appropriate to the situation at hand, but also the vocabulary and word-building skills have to be in place. Talking about a chrysalis to a three-year-old child is not going to be helpful; neither is reading *The Very Hungry Caterpillar* to a sixth-grade science class. The goal of our particular teaching lesson, however, is not only for a child to put out a leaf for a caterpillar to eat or to spell chrysalis correctly, but also to come to recognize the beauty of God in creation while living an environmentally sustainable life. The immediate goals should help the long-term one. Focusing exclusively on the easy wins can lead us to forget the difficult place we need to be going.

Using the analogy a little bit differently, we might compare preaching to law students learning the legal language. While they have to work with specific cases and statutes, the particulars are all in the service of forming lawyers that will have the right capacities, approach, and skills. No one, however diligent, can memorize all the laws, and many of them will be modified by legislatures after those students have graduated. Nevertheless, knowing how to write a brief, where to find relevant precedents, and how to handle various proceedings are all the fruit of intense study sessions, even though the specific details may never be encountered again.

One central outcome of giving people a new language is that they are able to use it. Children on the playground can look for and talk about caterpillars, and lawyers can go to court. Christians who hear a sermon about a new aspect of their walk of faith can talk about it together. Too many coffee hour conversations are restricted in their themes because people's understanding of church is limited to making sure the children have a good Sunday school or that enough money is raised to fix the roof. When the sermons begin a sustained discussion of topics like stewardship, or evangelism, or Christian conflict resolution, the people in the pews are given the language and the permission they need to have conversations about those subjects. What is acceptable to talk about has expanded. Those informal discussions are powerful mechanisms for the deepening faith and developing practices necessary to effect change. To me, the most striking effect of the long-term sermon is listening to parishioners using the new language learned to express their own understanding of what the church is about.

Thinking about preaching in this way is not new. What I am describing is the basic formation process. Paul expressed a similar sentiment when he talked about feeding people milk instead of solid food. Babies start with milk and eventually grow to the point of eating cereal, and then a whole range of solid food. But the process takes time. Trying to share a delicious steak with a baby just makes the baby sick (and wastes the steak). No one weaning a baby is planning to see a significant change in only one week, but the transition to solid food has to be made.

I am talking about preaching to help people learn how to eat solid spiritual food. I have not seen the discipline of preaching looked at in this particular way, although I assume others have thought about it. The books that deal with planning out sermons over the course of the year use a different approach and a slightly different set of goals. What I have found important is a long-term understanding of preaching that uses sermons over the course of more than a year to help a congregation move in a specific direction.

I see preaching, especially by the senior or lead pastor, as an essential component to congregational growth and development. As people's lives get busier, the sermon in Sunday worship is *the* time people are willing to listen to something important. They may not attend a meeting or read an e-mail, but when they are in church, they pay attention to a good sermon. In today's church environment, any significant attempt to change without a preaching strategy is likely to fail.

Using a long-term preaching strategy does not mean ignoring a church's lectionary, engaging in forced readings of scripture, or preaching only on one topic. Regardless of the congregation's focus, preachers still need to cover an array of scriptural, ethical, and doctrinal subjects. Amid those sermons, however, an extended sermon strategy encourages preachers to find a way to insert a few minutes about the long-term goal into every sermon. Such inclusion may make the sermon less rhetorically tight or include detours from a single, unified focus. Most congregants listening to the same person preach every week, though, will be much more responsive to intentional formation over time than a series of perfect homiletical events.

Another way of thinking about the long-term sermon in the midst of weekly preaching is to compare it to a series of family road trips. Our family has driven a number of times from western Pennsylvania to southern Alabama. Each trip had a particular, and sometimes significant, focus. If we didn't get to Alabama, the trip would have been a failure. That was the point. The ultimate destination. But we also wanted to use the trips to give our children new experiences along the way. One journey included a stop to Mammoth Cave in Kentucky. Another time we visited Nashville's Parthenon. Even if these experiences were a minor detour, they broadened our children's horizons and became part of our family's memories, helping us bond. We arrived at our destination a little bit later, but we were able to incorporate something important along the way.

To give a flavor of what I am talking about, I want to describe a two-year period in the parish where we decided to focus on increasing our passionate spirituality. In my parish, we came to realize that parishioners' lack of dedication to their own personal devotional lives was the primary issue holding us back as a congregation. Everyone loved coming together for worship and outreach and fellowship and anything else that happened at the church. But when they went home, they left their spirituality behind. The number of people reading the Bible, saying daily prayers, interceding for one another, or engaging in similar Christian practices was low.

The approach I took in preaching was to talk about spiritual practices frequently and repeatedly. One week, when the readings had a biblical character asking advice from another, I talked about spiritual direction and spiritual friendship. During a different week's reading on repentance, I talked about the practice of confession, including confession to other laypeople—which is acceptable in my tradition—and how it worked. I'm not sure that anyone went out and got a spiritual director that week, and I know that no one approached me for confession. In neither of those weeks was spiritual direction or confession the theme of the sermon. Instead, each was a slightly extended example of one way that the themes of the reading could be put into practice. Out of a fourteen-minute sermon, they were two- to three-minute asides meant to highlight ways that the spiritual life could be lived out in community on a day besides Sunday. My hope was that people would see that spiritual practices involving other people in a setting outside of the church facilities were a normal part of the Christian life. Unless those whose understanding of faith meant going to the church had heard enough examples of faith experiences happening in other places, they would never see it as applicable to them or try it for themselves. These examples might be repeated once or twice during the long-term sermon to reinforce the idea. Repetition at different times is also necessary to reach people who are away for a week, or in Florida for a season, or otherwise less regular in their attendance than a preacher would prefer.

While some examples during that time focused on spiritual intimacy with another Christian, other sermon pieces highlighted personal spiritual disciplines. Jesus's own prayer life was mentioned frequently, along with various concrete prayer practices paralleling Jesus's example. Different kinds of daily Bible reading methods were described, including the Daily Office, a read-the-Bible-in-a-year calendar, and *The Story*, which is a compilation of the Bible's greatest hits. The overall focus of most of these sermons was not on a spiritual discipline, yet I chose a scripture reading that described a particular devotion and took a few minutes to talk about it in more detail as an aside. Since the parish as whole was looking at the topic, the parish's Sunday morning adult group read through *The Story* and someone on staff led a read-the-Bible-in-a-year discussion. Some weeks, just being able to connect the lectionary reading with something going on in a small group discussion was enough to put the idea into people's heads that this was an important Christian practice.

One other initiative some parish leaders embarked on during that year was becoming what they called "spiritual trainers." They wanted to gain enough experience of prayer disciplines that they could help others pray better. Every two weeks they met to learn and to practice. Working the prayer practices the spiritual trainers group had studied that week into the sermon was a natural way to teach and reinforce a new language. While some leaders had been introduced to a practice, most of the congregation had not. By mentioning it in a sermon, not only did everyone hear about it, but those more experienced with the prayer discipline had an opening to talk about it at coffee hour or in other contexts. Even though most people did not begin to engage a particular practice, and often no one did, a variety of important things happened.

First, most people began to see deeper spiritual practice as normal for them and normal for their church. Many long-term Christians have many things that they believe they "should" be doing, but they aren't seen as important enough to them or their congregation to actually begin. By preaching over time about spiritual practices, everybody got the message that their relationship with God had a component that happened outside of church. Different people took that message in different ways. Some just felt slightly guiltier for ignoring it, but their attitude still changed.

Second, how people talked about spirituality at church transformed and deepened. At the end of the two years we focused on spirituality, people expected prayer to occur at meetings where it was previously absent. Parishioners became more comfortable asking each other for prayer, even at coffee hour or in informal settings. Spiritual practices and spiritual growth became normal topics of conversation for the parish leadership and were seen as an integral part of a healthy church.

Third, those who were ready to engage a deeper prayer life found the opportunities and the tools they needed, and in some cases new practices really took off. A group of people began "prayerwalking" and praying for the greater community. A healing team was founded and prayed for people after services. After the first read-the-Bible-in-a-year group finished with only two people making it through the entire year, someone else started a read-the-Bible-in-a-year Facebook group. For me this felt like a huge win because the person starting it was not someone I would have pegged as the next person to do a Bible study and because it happened after we had stopped intentionally focusing on spirituality. The change in understanding we hoped to see was manifesting itself in the congregation. People had learned a "new language."

The ideas in this book come out of my experiences as a solo pastor who preached almost every week. Thinking about preaching as a series of long-term term sermons to teach the congregation a new language is particularly important in congregations with a solo pastor. Most of them are small- to medium-sized churches with established congregations. The pastor wears many hats and has personal relationships with most congregants. The preacher also has the advantage of preaching almost every week with the discretion to focus those sermons freely. The preacher is an integral leader in almost every aspect of the church's life. In such a context, the practice of using long-term sermons is easily accepted by the congregation and a gift to preachers as they prepare their weekly message. Since the preacher knows the strengths and weaknesses of the parish, they are also the best person in the parish to choose the long-term sermon focus, even if the process of making that choice involves other leaders.

In a church with multiple regular preachers, these ideas are still effective. They will require more coordination and involve a discipline from all preachers to shape their weekly sermons in service of the larger goal, even if they were not involved in choosing that goal. Our congregations are not going to get where they need to go unless we are willing at every level to give up some of our autonomy to work collaboratively and to be accountable to other Christian leaders.

In their book *Rebuilt*, Michael White and Tom Corcoran describe the process of revitalizing their multistaff Roman Catholic church. One of their key learnings was the importance of preaching in feeding people. When they looked at themselves, however, they saw incredible inconstancies in quality and substance. With multiple services each week, and frequent guest preachers, they realized they had given up their prime opportunity to lead their congregation with no expectations or quality control.[4] They moved their church to a "one church, one message" approach where everyone preaching on any given weekend was covering the same themes in their homilies, and often those messages were parts of sermon series.[5] White and Corcoran suggest that the preachers and other church leaders are invited into the process of determining the focus of sermon series.[6] When they took their preaching more seriously, White and Corcoran saw significant church growth. They did not use the long-term sermon concept, but their approach to sermons series and involvement of multiple preachers, including guest preachers, provides a model for using the concepts in this book for larger parishes. While the

---

4. Michael White and Tom Corcoran, *Rebuilt: Awakening the Faithful, Reaching the Lost, and Making Church Matter* (Notre Dame, IN: Ave Maria Press, 2013).
5. White and Corcoran, *Rebuilt*, 142–43.
6. White and Corcoran, *Rebuilt*, 148.

implementation details may change a bit, the important work of leading a congregation through intentional, consistent preaching into long-term change applies to all churches.

Questions for Reflection and Discussion

- What in this chapter made you think about preaching in a different way?
- When in your ministry have you stopped too soon in sharing a vision that was needed for change?
- What is the longest you have ever maintained a preaching focus?
- In what ways does the analogy of preaching as learning a new language resonate with you? In what ways is it challenging?
- What experiences have you had of coordinating sermons with other preachers or of getting input about sermon themes from congregants?

Practical Exercises

- Think about an important change you would like to see in your congregation. Find a way to insert a two-minute segment that would help the congregation with that change into your next sermon.
- Ask your vestry or board what themes they think are most important for you to preach about in the coming weeks.

Imparting New Language Elements

All scripture is inspired by God and is useful for teaching, for reproof, for correction, and for training in righteousness.

—2 Timothy 3:16

I KNEW I HAD to be creative. I was starting my new call in August. The vestry had impressed upon me the need to develop the congregation's stewardship. The senior warden reinforced their emphasis by privately expressing concerns about being able to pay my salary after eighteen months unless something changed. Nobody, however, wants to hear the new preacher start begging for money out of the gate, nor does a winsome vision for the future start by focusing on financial fears. Most members of the parish had made pledges for the current year in November and were not likely to change them in the middle of summer. Confronting the issue immediately did not look promising.

I knew that stewardship development was more about fostering faith in the abundance of God than running a successful fundraising campaign. I decided that I could begin that work immediately if I approached it creatively. Rather than worry about how much people could give, I inserted topics into the sermons that the congregation would need if they were going to make more faithful pledges the coming November.

My first Sunday, the lectionary epistle reading was James 1:17–27, which contains an interesting phrase that in another context I probably would not have focused on. The end of verse 18 reads, "that we would become a kind of first fruits of his creatures." Understanding this phrase required an understanding of the Old Testament concept of first fruits giving, and I believe first fruits giving is key to faithful stewardship.

That morning, I spent about 40 percent of the sermon explaining what first fruits giving meant in scripture, how the concept is generally used today for tithing, and what that might have to do with us being the first fruits of God's creatures. From that explanation, I moved onto the central points of the James reading. While preaching the text of the day, I began the process of teaching the congregation the essential vocabulary of the language of stewardship.

The following week's gospel was the passage about Jesus and the Syrophoenician woman whose daughter was possessed by a demon, followed by Jesus's healing of a deaf man in the Decapolis. This reading is a difficult one to preach. Part of how I handled it, with stewardship in mind, was looking at the way we are challenged to share what we have. Jesus became willing to share his gifts with those who were not his people, eventually trusting that he could minister to all. I related that to our ability to trust in God's abundance as we share what we have, even with outsiders and those whom society may not deem worthy. That provided me a way to highlight the work of the food pantry and the generous gifts the congregation made to ensure our neighbors had enough to eat. The primary sermon focus challenged people to deeper relationships and conversion of heart toward the other, but I was able to weave in one significant stewardship theme.

I continued this basic approach the next two months.

When the reading from James included, "You do not have, because you do not ask. You ask and do not receive, because you ask wrongly" (4:2b–3a), the verses allowed me to spend about four minutes contrasting churches that ask God for new people to meet the budget and keep things the same versus those that ask God for new people to share our faith with and to prioritize our ability to do mission. Two weeks after that I included "withholding our tithes and offerings from God's storehouse" in a list of sins as part of a sermon on God's forgiveness and redemption. The following week's gospel, on the rich man instructed to sell all he had and give to the poor, was a natural place to talk about money and discipleship.

Intentionality about stewardship throughout the late summer and early fall meant that when the traditional stewardship season rolled around in November, the congregation had already heard more about tithing and faithful generosity than they had over the past few years. I brought this extended sermon focus to its peak with a three-week stewardship sermon series, which was also new to the congregation. That coincided with the annual stewardship letter, inviting people to put their pledge cards for the following year in the offering plate on the last Sunday of the series.

I took three disparate approaches for the three sermons. The first sermon covered the week's lectionary text on the widow's mite and focused on God's abundance. The second week, I requested permission from the bishop to use Malachi 3:7–12 as the first reading. Instead of focusing on the church's need for our money, I talked about our need to give and God's promises to take care of us when we are generous. Then, for the final week, I spent the sermon sharing my own stewardship journey, including my own significant struggles and setbacks as I learned to trust how God provided and cared for my family and me. I closed by sharing my family's pledge with the parish.

While not even close to an eighteen-month-long sermon, this extended four-month focus allowed the congregation to move forward. Pledges increased, and we got on a solid financial footing for the next year.

Taking the Time to Teach and Equip

Teaching a new language through preaching allows people to become comfortable with new concepts in discipleship before they are asked to begin applying them. Setting a copy of *War and Peace* in front of a third grader and making them feel guilty for not understanding it will neither aid their comprehension nor make them particularly interested in picking the book up later in life. Too often, we as preachers can be guilty of employing a similar pedagogy that is not only ineffective but also lacks love for our congregation. I have sat through sermons in failing congregations where preachers have guilted their people for not doing enough evangelism work, without sharing any tips, techniques, or perspectives on how that particular parish might be effective in sharing the Good News.

Churches almost always have some crisis happening, at least when viewed from a slightly anxious perspective. The temptation for church leadership is to want the issue of the moment solved immediately, and to start exhorting the congregation to drop everything and fix it. Important congregational transformation is unlikely to occur in a week or two, regardless of how impassioned the preaching, nor is serving the problem up with a large side of guilt on a Sunday morning likely to help matters.

Teaching a new language to move people toward a congregational goal is a better option than guilt because of the assumptions it makes about the people in our pews. Too many mediocre sermons assume that people both know how to do something and have the resources to do it, but still choose not to. A long-term sermon assumes that people want to move where God is calling the church but are unable to get there. Instead of being afraid that the church is refusing to do what is necessary, the long-term sermon trusts the congregation enough to believe that as they grow in their understanding and capacity—their faith—they will also make choices to grow in their discipleship. As the cultural incentives of church attendance have declined in recent decades, the congregations with us on Sunday morning deserve our trust. With fewer motivations to come to church outside of a desire for a deeper relationship with God, we can be confident that those present will take the right steps when they are able.

If we believe that people will move forward in discipleship when they are prepared, our sermon goal becomes preparing them to move in the direction that is currently most important for the health and growth of the church. To live into a new direction, the people in the pews will need some important information.

Elements a Congregation Needs to Make a Change

The first, and possibly most important, need for people to live into a change is to understand why that change is important. This understanding is essential before people make any change in their lives and is doubly important when that change involves something with the layers of personal importance, family history, and institutional authority as their church. Even early adopters and change agents in other areas are often more conservative about modifications in their church life and personal pieties.

Preaching about the importance of change usually covers a variety of areas. The most important is a vision of how things can look for the congregation and the larger community when the change is made. When a congregation has had a reasonable degree of success in the way things have always been done, painting a picture of how things could be better is essential. This understanding for change is a practical one. Hand-in-hand with the future vision, we must offer a description of ways that the current situation is not as good as it could be. Things may seem to be chugging right along, but many in the pews may not be aware of just how precarious things are. Or maybe what is happening is working well, but the community's needs have become so much greater that the church is no longer living into the fullness of its mission.

In addition to the practical, any change in a church context also has a spiritual motivation. Discipleship requires us to grow as individuals and as communities. God has a call for each congregation, and every church will undergo a variety of transformations to fully become what God has created it to be. A central preaching task is helping our people hear God's call through illuminating scriptural connections and the spiritual stories of the congregation itself. This spiritual underpinning is a key motivation for any change that will happen in the church context.

In addition to understanding why they need to change, people also need to know how to change. Teaching people how to make needed changes is, in some ways, a newer requirement of our preaching. In the past, preachers could expect that large portions of the congregation were able to learn something that they needed to know by attending church school sessions, parish meetings, and congregational trainings or other gatherings. Today in many congregations, the best or even only chance to teach a large percentage of the church is during the sermon; key leaders may not avail themselves of other opportunities. Even if the topics seem less "spiritual," using sermon time to look at the practical way to implement a change may be essential for a church to live into God's call. We can no longer afford the luxury of limiting the subject matter of our sermons when God is trying to get our people to grow.

Teaching people how to do something does, of course, includes a spiritual component. Talking about how to pray and create the spiritual momentum for congregational growth is essential. An important part of teaching people how to move forward is helping them understand that even the practical aspects of any changes are going to be done by cooperating with the work God is already doing. That spiritual emphasis may be paired with any variety of practical skills. Depending on the current focus, helpful sermons may walk people through putting prayer apps on their smartphones, giving people practice in naming a place they saw God working in their lives recently and sharing those God-sightings with someone else, or discussing the appropriate time to talk to someone on the vestry about a conflict in the church.

Addressing these topics is not something that can happen in a single morning sermon. Even a short series is likely inadequate to handle all aspects of what a congregation might need, although the sermon series can be a component of a larger initiative. A long-term sermon is the best approach to offer the needed theological rationale, practical vision, and concrete skills at an appropriate pace.

The goal of the long-term sermon is to allow time for the variety of information and application needed for a congregation to understand, get comfortable with, and be prepared to make changes. Instead of moving directly through information, a long-term sermon allows a preacher to introduce something in a small way and then circle back a couple of times while weaving in other relevant information that illuminates and reinforces the overarching goal. Such a practice assumes that the congregation needs to hear something several times to become comfortable with it. Preaching a consistent focus over a year or two also acknowledges that the average congregant is not in church every Sunday. Points need to be repeated for everyone to hear them, but preachers can't just preach the same sermon over and over again until it reaches the whole congregation. If some key leaders miss a great sermon while traveling, that is a loss. If those same leaders miss a key point about the parish's current focus during their trip, the preacher needs to ensure that the point is reinforced at other times.

Long-Term Sermons Integrated into the Weekly Sermon

Preaching a long-term sermon means that the goals for our weekly sermons will be slightly different. In seminary, most of us were taught to have a tight, coherent sermon. Many books on preaching rightly emphasize the effectiveness of having a single point for each sermon so that listeners know exactly what they are hearing and what the sermon is asking them to do. Some successful preachers argue that even the traditional "three points and a poem" sermon contain two points and one poem too many. As people's attention spans shorten, a homiletic laser-focus is helpful.

While maintaining best practices in preaching is important, we also need to look at our sermons as contributing to something larger. A good comparison for a long-term sermon might be movie franchises like the

Marvel Cinematic Universe. Each individual film has to be coherent and excellent in its own right and on its own terms. No one mistakes Spider-Man or Ant-Man for the Guardians of the Galaxy. At the same time, each film contains content that moves the story of the entire franchise forward. In some cases, the whole movie plot is integral to the larger series. In other films, however, the plot may center on an unrelated escapade. Even in the seemingly tangential installments, however, something happens that connects to the wider picture. That connection could be a conversation, the introduction of a character, or even a short seemingly unrelated clip at the end of the credits. Both the film and the connection are important. A series of isolated great films will not move the overall story arc forward. Each story, even with different actors and directors, makes its own impact while serving the larger whole.

Sometimes our weekly sermon will dovetail perfectly with our overarching focus. The example above about the rich young ruler being told to sell all he has and give to the poor during a stewardship arc is a great example. Usually, however, the point of our sermon will not line up so precisely, especially if we are preaching from the lectionary. To move forward, we need to find ways to incorporate some aspect of our larger goal into the weekly goal.

Many weeks, some aspect of the scripture readings connects with where we want the congregation to move. If the focus is on welcoming and hospitality, perhaps a character in the Hebrew Scripture reading exhibits hospitality in an interesting way or the Epistle lesson touches tangentially on the theme. Highlighting it for a minute or two as the reading is preached doesn't detract from the sermon. Letting the camera linger a little longer supports the long-term goals without detracting from the coherence of the sermon. The ability to incorporate a long-term point can influence the direction of the current week's theme without dominating it.

Other weeks, the scriptural passages may seemingly have nothing to do with the long-term sermon goal. Those weeks offer a couple of options. The easiest is to ignore the long-term focus for a week and pick it up again the following week. Not everything can, or should, happen every week. Sometimes the Spirit is moving in a different direction and God is ultimately responsible for giving the congregation what it needs. Ignoring the long-term focus is not the only faithful option, however. Most congregations are willing to follow a preacher, especially a preacher who is their pastoral leader, in more than one direction on a Sunday.

Some weeks, a sermon allows for an aside. A homiletics teacher might reduce a sermon grade for such detours, but these digressions can be meaningful for a congregation. A preacher can, in effect, say, "Let me pause for a minute to look at something else that I think is important." If the main sermon can be tied up seamlessly around or in spite of the diversion, a congregation is probably willing to listen. Such asides can also happen at the beginning of a sermon in ways that do not interfere with the structure and impact of the week's message. I have frequently opened a sermon by saying that before I begin to talk about this week's gospel, I want to look at a particular thing that happened that week. When the introduction connects to something else in the parish or in recent sermons, such homiletical preludes can work. One effective technique is highlighting something in the parish that happened over the past week that embodied part of the long-term sermon theme. When the congregational activity corresponds to a point preached over the previous couple of weeks, finding a way to mention it is essential.

A final way of integrating part of the long-term sermon focus with the scriptural readings of the day is by preaching what amounts to two shorter sermons on the same morning. I have explicitly explained to the congregation that I was doing this on some occasions, while on others I have made a rather abrupt pivot using an admittedly inadequate segue. While this may seem to break all the rules, preaching two sermons back-to-back has a number of advantages. Primarily, such practice treats the biblical text with integrity while also honoring the need to deal with an important aspect of the congregation's life. The sermons need not be equal length, and I have done them with either sermon first. I can see how long I need to talk about something contributing to the long-term focus, and then start with those points or end with them, depending on the week's theme. Usually the biblical text either lends itself to a more expository sermon that I would more likely put first, or it has a strong application that I would want to end with.

Some of you may be horrified by reading the above paragraphs. I admit that I would have been extremely skeptical of these techniques before I was the senior pastor and primary preacher of a parish for an extended length of time. What I have found is that structuring sermons in these creative ways has allowed me to provide the congregation with the information and encouragement needed to move them forward, and to repeat that movement over a number of cycles. Rarely, if ever, have I personally been able to achieve those kinds of results by focusing exclusively on my weekly preaching message.

Scripture, the Lectionary, and Long-Term Sermons

Scripture has its own integrity, and that integrity must be honored. Therefore, one important aspect of preaching that I do not advocate changing is how we deal with the biblical text. Certainly, preachers preach sermons that move in different directions from the same text. The needs of the congregation are important in determining which direction a sermon will take. The polyvalence of the text does not mean that any sermon can be preached on any text, however, nor does a long-term sermon focus provide an excuse for isogesis or sloppy scripture study. As preachers, we need to engage the text on its own terms before we bring our own needs and the needs of our congregation to it.

Even well-discerned needs, chosen in prayerful collaboration with the entire congregation, are still not an excuse to play fast and loose with the Word of God. Part of why I believe that asides, detours, or even sharing two sermons at once can be helpful is that we need to be clear what is part of the exposition and application of a scriptural passage and what is not. I would much rather say, "Our gospel reading says this; I also believe that is important," than to say, "Our gospel reading says this and sort of, kind of says that if you stretch it almost or just past the breaking point." Be clear about the distinction between what the Bible says and what the preacher says.

A long-term preaching focus does not supersede the lectionary for denominations like the Episcopal Church that use a lectionary for their scriptural readings and preaching texts, nor does it override other elements of the liturgical year. The lectionary's strength is the ability to move through a variety of topics that a preacher might otherwise forget about or ignore. The liturgical year also ensures that all the important points of salvation history and the life of Christ are celebrated and emphasized. The church, in its wisdom, has provided these cycles to prevent preachers from focusing solely on their current great idea while ignoring everything else. Congregations need to hear sermons covering a wide variety of scripture, doctrine, and spiritual discipline on a regular basis, even while they may be consistently learning a new language in a particular area.

One or more of the lectionary texts will likely determine the focus for the sermon of the week. The texts from the lectionary will also be read out loud to the congregation in almost all cases. Even if, for some reason, the preacher decides to preach on a theme not covered by the lectionary texts, the people still hear the scripture readings themselves. Preaching on a theme not stemming from the readings is rarely helpful. For me, I have limited such preaching to congregational events like the Stewardship Sunday or Annual Meeting Sunday, or in response to an external event such as the bombing of African American churches or a rancorous election. In some rare cases, I have asked for permission from the bishop to substitute one of the lectionary readings to preach on a particular text, as I did with Malachi during a stewardship series. Again, I do this rarely and try to maintain the lectionary readings so the congregation still hears them. Even using the lectionary, I have been able to preach extended sermons consistently.

Questions for Reflection and Discussion

- What aspects of the extended stewardship sermon discussion struck you? Did any of the choices make you uncomfortable?
- What do you see as the advantages and disadvantages of breaking traditional homiletical guidelines in favor of incorporating long-term sermon material?
- Are there particular times you think congregations need to hear practical visions of the future, theological rationales for change, or instructions for developing specific skills and practices?
- What are the strengths and weaknesses of lectionary preaching? How might those weaknesses be ameliorated through an extended sermon focus?
- Think about a time you have preached on something besides the scripture passages appointed for the day. What motivated your choice? What fruit came from that choice?

Practical Exercises

- Think about a change you would like to see in your congregation. Write down the practical vision of how things would be different if the change were made, the theological rationale for why God is calling the congregation to a new place, and the practical skills the congregation needs in order to move forward.
- Review some past sermons you have preached or heard. Find some assumptions made about the congregation's understanding or capacity that may not have been accurate and outline a better approach for that sermon.

– 3 –

Providing Theological Rationale and Practical Vision

For surely I know the plans I have for you, says the LORD, plans for your welfare and not for harm, to give you a future with hope.

—Jeremiah 29:11

PART OF THE ROLE of a long-range sermon is to provide hope for the future. Once we have discerned God is calling the congregation to move in a certain direction, we have to communicate that call in ways that are encouraging and hopeful. Like Jeremiah's words to the exiles, our extended sermon needs to find ways to help our church understand the importance of where they are going and begin to see what life might look like when they get there. We don't have to have all the answers, but doing our work well will entice the congregation to live into those transforming answers themselves.

Theological Rationale

Thinking about the theological reasons for a change is easy for preachers. They dovetail nicely with the focus of most sermons. We regularly draw on the scriptures to provide a vision for some aspect of the reign of God that speaks to the needs and yearnings of the congregation. We demonstrate how scriptural stories and instruction prod us to live in certain ways that benefit us and those around us. We offer theological perspectives on the issues of the day and the difficult decisions being made by individuals and families in our context. The primary change in moving from a weekly sermon focus to a long-term sermon focus is not so much what we are doing but finding ways to consistently return to the same topic over time.

The concrete elements we use to preach a theological or moral rationale for the necessary change will vary depending on the scriptures for the week. Sometimes we are blessed with the widow's mite reading during stewardship season or Matthew 18 while talking about conflict resolution. Other times, we might depend more on asides that draw out aspects of numerous texts and slowly build up over time. A focus on spiritual disciplines, for example, can highlight examples of Elijah fasting, or explain why John's disciples fasted and Jesus's did not, while noting the variety of ways that Jesus was in relationship with the Father and the disciples maintained their relationship with Jesus. A focus on spiritual gifts can certainly draw on Paul's letters, but may also find good examples of different gifts exhibited by various disciples or figures from the Hebrew Bible. Spending a couple of minutes discussing how Jesus encounters unfamiliar people with generosity and grace can make an easy link to an evangelism focus. The rest of that day's sermon can continue with the other aspects of the reading, but the long-term focus will have been advanced.

A scriptural prodding critical of the current situation can also help motivate a needed change. The idea is not to lay on guilt, but to help people come to realize the serious problems of failing to live into Jesus's call for them.

Congregations, like all of us, are adept at rationalizing away their own particular sins and failings. A lack of evangelism can be laughed off for God's "frozen chosen." A culture of backbiting and gossip can be dismissed as "just who we are." Not supporting each other in prayer and not stopping to deepen relationships with other parishioners is excused since everyone is too busy. In the midst of such concrete congregational problems, a preacher is going to find ways to say over and over that such a situation is not what God wants for that church.

We might find Paul talking about an analogous issue to our church's in one of his letters, or in another scriptural reading for the day. More frequently, however, we will have to find ways to continue to highlight the issue. One simple way is to include the current issue in a preacher's list. Most of us have reason from time to time to include in a sermon a list of ways that the world around us is broken, sinful, and in need of healing. When gossip or lack of hospitality shows up next to murder and drug overdoses, our listeners have a sense that they might need to pay more attention to their behavior than previously thought. Simply including something, without comment, in such a list allows the congregation to accept it as they are ready, or as the Holy Spirit deems right to convict them at a deeper level. A couple of such mentions over the course of a few months, combined with coming at the focus from other directions, can slowly change people's perceptions. Instead of trying to force a congregation to come along all at once, preachers can allow them to come along at their own pace. The goal is to give people "aha" moments that motivate change instead of moments of guilt that spur resistance.

Pushing a little harder than the preacher's list, a scriptural message that focuses on healing, forgiveness, restoration, or salvation may include a couple of concrete examples of ways that God's love brings transformation and change. We know that Jesus healed lepers and reached out to Samaritans, and we can assure our people that he also cares enough to help us with our current congregational focus, whether that focus is making time for personal prayer, overcoming bitterness in the congregation, or opening our worship to children. As a church sees its struggles as something that God wants to liberate them from as much as Jesus offered healing and salvation to those in his earthly ministry, its willingness to engage the next steps of the process increases.

Practical Vision

In addition to the theological motivation for change, the congregation will also need practical ones. Practical motivation for change comes from both a vision for the future and from discomfort with the current situation.

Often when we think about vision casting, our minds may go to an overarching theological or spiritual amalgamation of the end of the book of Revelation and Isaiah 2, 11, and 65. These eschatological visions are important, but so are the practical images of what church life could be like here and now if we made the changes proposed by the long-term sermon focus.

In *The Practice of Adaptive Leadership,* Ronald Heifetz, Alexander Grashow, and Marty Linsky talk about the importance of a vision in order to keep people from defaulting to their existing interpretations. Their insights from the secular business world apply equally to congregations. Churches, especially declining churches, have many unhelpful explanations. Heifetz writes that "often the default interpretations . . . conveniently serve to shield them from the need for them to change."[1] When I got to St. John's, the Sunday attendance had been declining for some time. The shared interpretations for the decline put it out of the congregation's control. These interpretations included the area's

---

1. Ronald Heifetz, Alexander Grashow, and Marty Linsky, *The Practice of Adaptive Leadership: Tools and Tactics for Changing Your Organization and the World* (Boston, MA: Harvard Business School Press, 2009), 113.

population loss and the decision of the Episcopal Church to move forward with same-sex blessings and ordinations. What the congregation was not able to see were the ways that their own decision to move from two priests to one combined with an understandable lull following a significant capital campaign also influenced attendance. The narrative the church told itself was that decline was inevitable, and therefore change was unnecessary. Until the congregation heard and accepted a different vision, any change was going to be thwarted.

Another common default in established churches is to harken back to past periods that seemed more successful, at least in hindsight. If we believe that the same programs done in the same way will again foster growth, significant change is unnecessary. For years St. John's held a children's chapel service in a beautifully appointed room in the basement. Someone had built a child-sized altar space, complete with altar, altar rail, and wooden chairs for preschoolers. Two boxed stained-glass windows were installed in the windowsills, and the chapel even had its own organ. The space was created with great care and was a truly beautiful room for children to have a liturgical worship experience. Over the past decade, however, the basement had become unsuitable for the chapel. Most of it was used by the food pantry, and parents had little tolerance for sending their children off to a basement that was cold in the winter and difficult to access from the primary worship space. As long as the default interpretation of a thriving church meant filling that chapel with children, two significant ministries were stuck. We decided, however, to allow the food pantry to use the space for a clothing closet and to move the children's chapel to an upstairs space off the lounge where parents gathered for coffee hour. Tearing apart the woodwork was not an easy decision, but it was the right one. We could move the altar itself and the chairs upstairs, but some of the overall beauty of what had been was lost.

This decision to change the children's chapel could only have been made because people saw a different future for the church. The new vision included a growing food pantry that provided clothing as well as food to those in need in our community and a children's ministry with families who wanted something different than what many of the current parishioners had experienced.

Part of that change happened as I lifted up a different vision over the course of an extended sermon. I never preached on getting rid of the children's chapel. I did talk about the ways that the parish could grow and thrive by meeting the needs of those around us in different ways. When gospel parables about feeding the hungry and clothing the naked arose, I emphasized the needs of our downtown neighbors. This emphasis included God's call for us to assist them, but also included a vision of a growing church where our neighbors became part of our parish and not just its outreach clients. As this vision was proclaimed, two shifts were able to happen.

The first shift was that people who had been clinging to the default explanations began to hear that another way was possible. Well before difficult decisions came before the church board, everyone was introduced to a new way of thinking about what the congregation might look like. Some people quickly discarded the default interpretations in favor of more hopeful ones, others went back and forth depending on the day, and still others remain a bit skeptical years later.

The second shift that preaching a new practical vision facilitated was freeing people who had already been looking toward that vision to act. Just because a default interpretation was prevalent did not mean it was universally accepted. Lifting up an alternative vision gave people who were hungry for such a vision the permission to move on it. If they were hearing their hopes and dreams for the parish articulated in the pulpit, then they probably had permission to live out those dreams in their ministries. As people are given permission for their best aspirations for the congregation, transformation begins.

Preaching a practical vision for the parish means illustrating a future that could happen, while recognizing it is not the final word. Heifetz writes, "Effective visions have accuracy. . . . Providing thoughtful, accurate interpretations that get at the essence of the complex reality you observe . . . is enormously helpful to people."[2] A congregation facing the adaptive challenges of a changing culture needs someone to provide a coherent vision that fits their particular circumstances.

John Kotter lists four elements of a transformational vision. First, a transformational vision is "ambitious enough to force people out of comfortable routines."[3] The vision we are preaching is not about making next year's budget but transforming our church and the wider community. Kotter's second point focuses on providing better products for a lower cost. This point might require some translation into a church context, since we aren't trying to provide the least expensive worship service in town. Recognizing that participation in our church life does involve various costs beyond financial ones is important. When our local high school Christmas concert conflicts with church choir rehearsal, we can lower the cost of participation by rescheduling. Offering a soft space for children during worship reduces the practical and emotional costs for parents who bring their little ones. Such cost reductions require changes in how the church operates, and making changes requires sharing a practical vision with the congregation.

Kotter's third element of a transformational vision is incorporating new trends such as globalization and technology. At a congregational level, this idea may mean casting a vision of a church that includes those from the neighborhood's changing demographics. A sermon inviting people to pull out their smartphones and check in on social media provides opportunities for members to think about how the church can use technology in different ways. Most of our congregation is looking for a way to understand how societal changes can be reconciled to their understanding of church and are grateful when such a vision is provided.

---

2. Heifetz, Grashow, and Linsky, *Practice of Adaptive Leadership*, 113.
3. John Kotter, *Leading Change* (Boston, MA: Harvard Business School Press, 1996), 79.

Kotter's final point is that the vision is nonexploitative and, thus, has moral power.[4] Any authentic vision we preach is going to inclusive and uplifting. Churches offer people the opportunity to see the world around them in moral dimensions. Our practical visions of the future touch the hearts of people longing for a more just and compassionate world. The preacher does the difficult work of providing such a vision so the congregation can respond. Their responses will likely range from acceptance to resistance to significant adaptation. Any response can be helpful, because the preacher is not going to go into their study alone to produce the final vision of what the congregation's future will look like. Preachers may put forth a first draft, or components of a first draft, in different sermons over a few months. Both Kotter and Heifetz note, however, that the vision will be influenced by others over time, who provide feedback in various settings, and their actions, whether positive or negative, will also influence the vision's next iteration.[5] Heifetz also advises humility in those of us casting visions. Instead of trying to come up with *the* interpretation of a future vision, we may want to set forth multiple ones. He suggests we audition our interpretations rather than advocate for them.[6]

The elements of a future practical vision that we audition will have themes that align with our long-term sermon focus, but details may change over time. A focus on getting the congregation to engage the community around them may talk about how the church might look with an expanded food pantry. The next month, the theme might be on revising youth programming to invite neighborhood children. Three weeks later, the topic might be welcoming unexpected visitors into worship. After hearing these ideas for six months, a few members of the congregation may decide to start a community meal. Such activity would count as a great success for the long-term sermon focus and the work

---

4. Kotter, *Leading Change*, 79.
5. Kotter, *Leading Change*, 81.
6. Heifetz, Grashow, and Linsky, *Practice of Adaptive Leadership*, 122.

of vision-casting. Those members were obviously listening. The details of the various visions might not have proven entirely accurate, but the preaching was heard.

In addition to painting a picture of what a transformed future might look like, the extended sermon will also include a description of problematic aspects of the current reality. These difficulties might stem from challenges within the congregation, changes in the local community, or issues arising in the broader society. In some ways, this diagnosis of the current realities facing the congregation comes before the work of creating a future vision. The information gleaned from a solid assessment is essential for the focus of the long-term sermon.

Incorporating the problems necessitating change into sermons can be tricky, however. Lifting up what is really happening can be an essential motivator. Especially if many in the congregation default to memories of the way things were in the past when they were more involved, being clear about where the congregation is today is essential. At the same time, that reality must be good news to be proclaimed in the pulpit. Wallowing in problems without resolving them can lead to despair. Expounding challenges in excruciating detail then offering a simple, magical-thinking solution will not motivate people to positive action either.

Importantly, focusing exclusively on problems is not an accurate diagnosis of any situation. No congregation is made up solely of issues. Every congregation has gifts and assets as well. Knowing the right way to weave the issues with the assets is the art of teaching people a language about their congregational life that helps them move forward. Such work is the goal of a long-term sermon.

Coupling issues with opportunities for growth does not mean shying away from saying difficult things. In some ways, naming the problems will be easily received, because people are already aware of them. The congregation probably knows at least as well as the preacher that there are not as many children in Sunday school or that the neighborhood around the church is now impoverished or that people are not treating each other like Christians. What they may not know is that they also have the capacity to squarely face these issues head on. Fear, avoidance, and resigned acceptance can all maintain their hold if nothing is never named, but if only the negatives are named, then people can feel justified in maintaining their current mindset. When the issues are named and then relativized by the ways that God has worked through the parish in the past or by the congregation's capacity for renewal, people can begin to see the issues in a new light.

As we hear about Jesus welcoming the little children, the preacher can both note how few children are currently in the nursery and recognize the strengths the congregation has always brought to this ministry and the number of babies in the community. The end of that sermon section might be a set of visionary ellipses that proclaims a belief in the parish's ability to turn the current situation around even if there is not a solution yet. A parish experiencing burnout might have that exhaustion named by the preacher alongside of a long-term focus on spiritual gifts. That sermon could then note that the congregation has the gifts to do what God is calling them to do, but they may need to reorganize and simplify its work in response to that call. Complaints about the increasing number of people in the community not coming to church can be recognized along with the evangelism opportunities such a situation provides once the congregation prepares itself to do that work.

Another way the pastor can practically motivate a congregation is by highlighting what is happening in the wider community. The more a congregation sees itself as part of the solution to the problems of their neighborhood or world, the more likely they will be willing to do the hard work of change. Many stories of congregational turnarounds involve a transformation from an inward focus to an outward focus. More commonly, however, congregations have a balanced focus and need to hear what is happening on the edges of their current ministries. Instead of changing everything, they need a better understanding of what is happening just beyond what they currently see, and what direction they may need to go to meet those needs. Being able to share this information with the congregation means that the preacher will be engaged with the wider community. That exact engagement will be different depending on the preacher and the congregation, and it may focus on the immediate neighborhood, on missionary work in other parts of the world, or in social justice activities in the surrounding communities.

A few years ago, while I was in the midst of a long-term sermon on loving relationships, a young black man, Michael Brown, was shot by a white police officer in Ferguson, Missouri. In the aftermath of that tragedy, the local Presbyterian minister invited a diverse representation of area pastors to meet with four local chiefs of police. Over a series of four meetings we were able to share a variety of information and experience. As part of those meetings, one of the local African American pastors talked about what he wished his white siblings would preach in their congregations. He related some of his stories of explicit racism as a municipal employee, as well as systemic issues that African Americans in our community faced. I was able stand up in my predominantly white parish the next week and share what he had said. Some of his points were not ones I could have preached on my own because they were not in my own experience. Having permission and encouragement from him to tell his story allowed me to share it with my congregation on Sunday morning even as he stood in his own pulpit less than two miles away. While most of the focus on loving relationships during the two years of that extended sermon focused on how our congregation treated each other, this community issue expanded that focus.

Part of the practical consequence of that sermon was that both I and the congregation had a stronger understanding of our need to be in closer relationship with the African American churches in our community. Our congregation decided to take a field trip on a Sunday morning. We shortened our normal 10:00 am service to 45 minutes and then drove to the 11:00 am service of my colleague's church. Not everyone came, of course, but enough people did to begin to build relationships. Later that winter, we joined their church for a Watch Night service on

New Year's Eve. Participating in that service provided an opportunity to teach our congregation about the African American tradition of Watch Night services stemming from when slaves stayed up all night on New Year's Eve in 1862 waiting for the announcement of the Emancipation Proclamation and their freedom. Our congregations have joined each other a couple of times since, with good, and sometimes difficult, work being done through our relationship.

This experience is a good example of the kind of fruit that can be born from a long-term sermon. I was preaching about loving relationships, on a variety of levels, including how to interact with and love people who we saw as different or held different perspectives. God opened up a door for us that we were prepared to walk through based on the work we were doing. The results were not what I and the church health team that worked on identifying our focus had expected. Yet what happened was important on a variety of levels and deepened the congregation's ability to be in loving relationships within and outside of the parish.

Questions for Reflection and Discussion

- How did this chapter add to you thinking about how to motivate a congregation toward change?
- How has a preacher offering a theological rationale motivated you to change in the past?
- What ways do you generally offer a practical vision? Do you favor drawing a picture of the future, describing current problems in the church, or looking at the wider community? Do you find different aspects more helpful with different themes? Can you describe a time you put all the elements together?
- When has a congregation been motivated to make a change by your preaching? What elements were most important in inspiring that action?

Practical Exercises

- Write down the practical effects a positive change in your congregation would have. Describe the current problems and paint a picture of the church with those problems transformed into opportunities and blessings.
- Pick three teachings or parables of Jesus and show how they function as practical visions that motivate people to change.

– 4 –

Explaining How to Take the Next Steps

*Greet Prisca and Aquila, who work with me in Christ Jesus,
and who risked their necks for my life, to whom not only I
give thanks, but also all the churches of the Gentiles.*

—Romans 16:3–4

AT THE END OF Paul's letter to the Romans, a soaring theological treatise that has inspired libraries of books and fomented endless doctrinal disputes, we find a long list of greetings. Most have a short description of the people being greeted, sometimes with reasons that they are dear to Paul or ought to be received with honor by the church. Explaining this final chapter as a natural conclusion to a letter from someone who misses many he loves only captures one piece of Paul's motivation. He is also supremely concerned with the ongoing evangelical ministry and connection between his new churches. His greetings and introductions help ensure the success of that ministry. Paul wants the Romans

41

to know that nothing will ever separate them from the love of God in Christ Jesus (8:38–39). He also wants to make sure that the Romans will help the deacon Phoebe with whatever she needs to continue her work (16:1). Paul recognizes that connecting people in his churches is an important way to help them press on in their work for the gospel. Taking time at the end of his letter to mention people they might know and encourage them to further their work is one way to make those connections effectively.

The Importance of Teaching Change

Taking the time to teach a congregation the practical details of how to make a change happen might seem an unusual sermon focus, but such work is increasingly important. The busyness of modern life makes it difficult to find times when a large percentage of the congregation is available other than Sunday morning. Even if every Christian education class were willing and able to focus on the same practical teachings for a period of time, many congregational leaders would miss the teaching entirely. While a significant portion of the congregation will also miss worship on any given Sunday, part of the goal of a long-term sermon is to reinforce teachings in various ways over time. Sporadic attenders will encounter the theme and regulars hear enough to develop a new language in that area of faith and discipleship.

Teaching the practical how-to of change from the pulpit is also important for other reasons. When the pastor preaches about something, that topic gains an increased standing in the congregation. What is said in the sermon is put in the middle of congregational life, at least for that Sunday morning, to be discussed at coffee hour, in Sunday school classes, and in other settings. Those who want to run with what is taught are given the authorization to push onward, and those who might be unsure are given permission to experiment and even receive support and encouragement. Part of the power of this sermonic sanction stems from the congregation hearing the message together. A discussion can continue because I have heard what you have heard, and I heard you hear it too. This common experience is especially important as people try new skills and take risks for change. Seeing those in the pews around me learning the same things provides security that no one is in this alone. Such peer support, and maybe even a bit of positive peer pressure, fosters congregational transformation.

Another reason to offer practical teaching as part of the sermon is those in the pews increasingly come from a variety of religious traditions or even no tradition. If most of my congregation are Episcopalians who have attended the same church for decades, I may feel confident about what they have experienced and learned in church. When the majority of the congregation began attending in the past five years, I may have no idea what they know. This increasing variety of backgrounds offers at least two strengths, however, for lifting up the practical elements needed for change. The first is that some people may come from denominations or congregations where our current weakness is their strength. God is actually very good at sending such people when we need them to live into our calling. When the need for their expertise is highlighted in a sermon, they are encouraged to share what they know and offer leadership. Second, newer people are often still open to discovering what is important in their church home. By highlighting particular skills and activities, they may be motivated to dive in. People who are too new to know that "it was never done that way before" are a blessing to the change process.

The practical *how* that needs to be taught during a long-term sermon can include a wide variety of skills, activities, and practices. A congregation working on spiritual gifts may need to know what spiritual gifts are, how they work, how individuals can determine their spiritual gifts, and how ministries can recruit based on gifting instead of guilting. When our parish has worked on evangelism, part of the practical teaching in sermons involved helping people write out what excited them about their faith and then practice telling someone else. When we took a field trip to the African American Baptist congregation, our people needed to know a variety of details, including what they could expect from the service, how to get to the church, and how much to put into the collection plate. When working on the conflict resolution portion of our loving relationship focus, the sermon included practical instructions about talking to people directly when at odds with each other.

Practical Advice and Examples in Scripture and in the Congregation

These practical topics can be discussed in a variety of ways and using different approaches over the course of an extended sermon is helpful. The first place we can look for practical advice is scripture itself. Much of the Bible is focused on concrete ways to help congregations make the changes needed to live into God's call, whether that congregation is the people of Israel, the early church as a whole, or a specific church. Preaching often involves moving from explaining scripture to applying it, and by paying attention to our long-term sermon focus, we help people make important connections. We may also want to bring biblical wisdom into our sermons that might not be otherwise heard. Some books, like Proverbs, are full of practical wisdom, but rarely show up in liturgical church lectionaries. Other passages of scripture speak specifically to one issue, and we need to find a way for the congregation to hear them. I have found Malachi 3:8–12 helpful when talking about tithing. Those verses do not appear in our lectionary, however, so I have had to be intentional about finding ways to focus on them.

Another important way of highlighting how a change can be made is by making note when and where people in the congregation are engaged in transformed behaviors. The advantages of looking in the church are at least threefold. First, positive reinforcement is the best method for teaching and encouraging behavior modifications. Noticing a positive behavior during a sermon promotes the continuation of that behavior. Second, highlighting an example of where the long-term focus is finding success demonstrates to the rest of the congregation that transformation is possible. Instead of an unknown, scary hypothetical, people can see that someone they know tried something new and came out the other side in one piece. Third, people like to hear what others are doing in the parish. Just mentioning the successes of others connects people in good ways.

We can mention particular people in a number of ways for various reasons. When a long-term sermon focus is chosen with input from a group of congregational leaders, summarizing other parish work on the same focus is helpful. Discussing what Sunday school classes are learning when it aligns with the current focus is also good. When St. John's was working on passionate spirituality, one group tackled reading the Bible in a year and another group offered a "Lent Madness" competition.[1] Mentioning anything those groups learned over the week both helped people see such devotions as normative and provided practical ways that people could embark on them. When we focused on evangelism, one of our long-time parishioners spent six months praying for her best friend and repeatedly inviting her to come to church. Eventually she came on a Sunday morning, then she got more involved, and eventually joined the vestry. Five members of her family were baptized. The praying parishioner was not someone people immediately thought of when they heard the word "evangelist," yet she was one of our church's most effective ones. Finding a way to tell her story at the right time was important. Her work let the parish know that "normal" people like them could do effective evangelism. Changing the congregation's internal images of evangelism from the door-to-door salesman stereotype to seeing their introverted friends as evangelists was a huge step in our living into God's call.

---

1. See LentMadness.org for more information on Lent Madness.

Using Announcements

Some of the information worth highlighting any given week as part of a long-term sermon might fit more in the announcements than in the sermon. As I have experimented with preaching extended sermons, one of my realizations has been that often, important pieces of the sermon can occur outside of the sermon. The weekly announcements, in particular, can be used to lift up aspects of the current congregational focus. Using the announcements for what is important to the congregation probably seems almost self-evident. Using the announcements or other parts of the service in ways that complement the sermon—and the extended sermon—requires intentionality, however.

On a number of occasions, I have wanted to explain something happening in the parish in an extended way. The informality of the announcements, which in my context allows a different kind of give and take with the congregation than the sermon itself, has its advantages, especially if I want to acknowledge someone for their work in a way that includes a certificate or other recognition. If I am explaining something that has nothing to do with the week's sermon, I may also choose the announcement time. Depending on what my announcement plans are for the week, I may change the length of my sermon. I let people know at the beginning or at the end of the sermon what I am doing and why. Allowing the congregation to know what to expect helps keep their attention focused on what I am saying instead of trying to figure out what I am doing.

In some cases, I will make an announcement in the middle of the sermon when it is closely related to the theme of the week or corresponds to the long-term sermon focus. At a transition point, I stop and take an aside to tell people what is happening. Depending on the situation, I may even say something like this week's sermon is being sponsored by our parish food pantry, which will be packing bags after church. Such detours may not be model homiletical technique, but people are used to following a story with the occasional commercial break thrown in.

When the detour is in the service of a larger sermon focus, such asides allow a congregation to process other pieces of the sermon.

Parishioners Speaking

Another way to highlight the work of others in the congregation who are making progress on the long-term sermon focus is hearing directly from parishioners. Depending on the story they have to tell and their comfort level, they can be invited to preach, to come up for part of the sermon, or to speak during the announcements. Many churches invite members to talk about some aspect of their faith or ministry on a regular basis, and these moments can be powerful. Some clergy do interviews with a parishioner during the sermon or announcement time to let them tell their story without quite as much pressure.

Regardless of how congregants share their experiences, they need to feel supported and given every chance to succeed. Some are natural storytellers and will have the congregation begging for more. Others will be nervous and need opportunities to practice. Ensuring adequate amplification is also important. Even if some people regularly stand up and shout out announcements without a microphone, anyone telling their story should have one. Following up with a thank-you note or other encouragement is also important. Any preacher can feel insecure about what they said, and we have a responsibility to ensure that those we ask to share feel good about what they have done.

We also bear a responsibility whenever we highlight stories and examples from the congregation to use them appropriately. Obviously, we want people to feel honored and appreciated when their ministry is mentioned. One of my parishioners says that people's favorite sound is that of their own name when they are being thanked. When publicly talking about what someone has done, we want to be unfailingly positive and exceedingly enthusiastic. Be in full cheerleader mode with no hint of even constructive criticism or ambivalence. Selecting a variety of people from the congregation matters as well. Choosing people that come from different services, friendship groups, ministries, length of time as members, and demographic categories allows the entire congregation to relate to some people who are working on aspects of the current parish focus. Nobody wants to hear the same names all the time, even the people those names belong to.

Other Congregations

Sometimes the best practical examples come from outside the congregation. When another church makes an effective change in our current area of focus, I want our church to hear about it. The more the congregation can feel connected to that example the better. Another struggling church in the community with similar issues and demographics is ideal, but congregations in other parts of the country or the world that face similar issues can offer inspiration.

When talking about other congregations, a few things are important to keep in mind. Most significantly, examples should lift up those who are hearing the sermon, and not discourage or shame them. Getting excited about how well a growing, wealthy megachurch managed to do something is unlikely to give a struggling, pastoral-sized church a lot of hope. A sermon where the pastor offers the answer from another church that has done things more effectively is unlikely to encourage those who have been toiling away at the problem. Any hint that the preacher might prefer to work with the other church that has figured things out must be eliminated entirely. Instead, mention the other congregation with inquiry and wonder. Even when we are preaching something eminently practical, the sermon is still about good news. We want to say, "Wow, look at what happened over here! We might be able to learn something. Let's look at this together."

Remember that the sermon is first and foremost about what God is doing. If we are lifting up another church, the core of the good news is that God is working through these people to do something very much like what we feel God is calling us to do. We can encourage our congregation that God could work with us in the same way, and note that maybe God is giving us an opportunity to learn from them. The same focus on God and God's work in us applies anytime we use illustrations, including those from within our congregation. If something amazing is happening in our church, we want to help everyone, including those directly involved, to see that God is doing something with us. Such a focus is both theologically correct and practically effective. We are much more likely to answer God's call to change if we look for and cooperate in those circumstances where God is already engaging that transformation.

We as preachers may also have stories to tell about ways we have learned and grown in our long-term sermon focus. If the goals we and the congregation have discerned are going to be successful, we as leaders have to stretch and grow. The same caveats that apply to using examples from other people and congregations apply, however. Our focus has to be on how God has helped us learn and grow in ways that make everyone else in the congregation feel like God could help them learn and grow as well. Like many Episcopalian clergy, I have not thought of myself as a natural evangelist. When the parish focused on evangelism, I talked about my own fears and discomfort, pointed to examples of people I wanted to emulate, tried a risky new behavior, stumbled a bit, and watched God bless even my initial awkward attempts. Pointing to one or two concrete behaviors I attempted allowed me to teach them to the congregation as a comrade instead of as an expert. I could acknowledge, firsthand, that the changes were not easy ones to make, and assure everyone that we were in the struggle together.

Exercises during the Sermon

In some cases, teaching a practical skill means the sermon will look a lot like an unwieldy church school class, complete with handouts, worksheets, and practical exercises. Faith development may mean thinking about something, writing it down, and sharing it with another person. The preacher can tell people how to do that and ask them to do it on their own time, or the preacher can have the congregation complete the exercises during the sermon.

While I was working on welcoming and evangelism as a long-term sermon, one of the issues was engaging visitors during coffee hour. Like most people who enjoy being together, people from our parish tended to talk to each other when given the opportunity. On occasion, this meant that visitors were ignored. In order to look at this practical issue, I addressed three points in the sermon. The first was to make people aware of the problem, since we often don't realize when others feel excluded by our conversations. Then I wanted to give some concrete ways to talk to people we didn't know, since making coffee hour small talk can be difficult for some. Finally, I wanted to encourage people to connect a coffee hour guest with someone else in the parish. Welcome, engage, connect.

For Welcome, I worked with a few parishioners to do a short skit about a group of people having a private conversation and a visitor trying desperately to be included. It was over-the-top and funny, but it made the point. For Engage, I included a five-by-seven-inch card in the bulletin that had bubbles for people to fill in: "Good Things about St. John's," "Things about Yourself," and "Questions to Ask Someone." I walked the congregation through each section, explaining that these were easy things to talk to someone about at coffee hour. Then I encouraged them to make an introduction between the visitor and someone else. I finished the sermon by asking everyone to walk around the church, find someone they did not know very well, and talk to them about the things they had just written down. The energy at the end of the sermon was high. I had a hard time getting people back to their pews for the Nicene Creed. That sermon was one component of an extended sermon that made a difference in the life of the parish.

Sermon Series

One way to incorporate a number of these techniques is a sermon series. Making clear that a certain number of sermons are going to have a specific focus is a great way to make a push for change once the ideas in a long-term sermon have been discussed. Looking at one topic from multiple perspectives over an intensive period allows the congregation to focus on what our sermons have touched on in a more diffuse way.

For me, a sermon series works like the final baking of a loaf of bread. Basic, foundational ingredients are added to the dough and kneaded together at the beginning of the process. Then the dough is left to proof for a while. At the right time, other ingredients—fruit or items bringing special flavor and texture—are added, and the dough sits some more. These early mixings and proofings occur as we introduce different concepts and understandings over a long-term sermon series. Often, they represent our understanding of God's calling us to a new future and the vision for what that future could be. We also teach some of the practical pieces and highlight places where similar changes are occurring within and beyond the congregation. Then comes the time when we shape everything together and put it in the oven in preparation for the beautiful, warm, fragrant bread the entire process is designed to yield. In our extended sermon work, this final baking might be a sermon series. Taking a couple of weeks to reiterate what has been said and to teach the specific skills still to be learned can help the congregation live into the desired change. Just as bread is only going to be as good as the combination of its ingredients and the quality of its kneading and baking, the fruit of the long-term sermon is going to depend on the new language appropriated over time and the willingness to apply that language. Not every extended sermon focus needs to have a sermon series near its end. Some no-bake desserts work perfectly well. Yet the sermon series can be an important way to let the congregation know that the church is moving forward now and is inviting them along.

In my experience in a lectionary-based church where worship is organized around the liturgical year, sermon series between three and five weeks are the most effective. Less than three is really not a series, and more than five begins to lose people's attention. In a church that organizes its worship primarily by sermon topics or other means, a series will work differently. I have used sermon series effectively in Advent and Lent, when the congregation already sees those weeks in a particular way. Other times of the year also work, as long as the sequence is clear of significant events in the liturgical year or church life. I learned the hard way that a sermon series planned in January when snow and ice storms interrupt attendance is not ideal.

A couple of components contribute to the effectiveness of a sermon series. The first is the congregation's awareness that a series is coming. I often let my vestry know my plan and get their buy-in, and then advertise it in the congregation. Simple things like newsletter and bulletin articles raise awareness. I want people to know the sermon series is happening. Even if they miss all the sermons, they still know that the parish thought it was an important emphasis. Those who are active in the parish, and especially active in its planning and leadership, will hopefully make an effort to be present.

Second, in a sermon series I am more intentional about using the gifts and expertise of others in the congregation. Utilizing people's gifts is always a good idea. As a solo pastor, however, I find that I do not have the time to engage the congregation fully in assisting with the preparation of every sermon. I can make that time on occasion, however, and I want to make those occasions count. Sometimes incorporating others involves a short skit, as in my earlier example. Sometimes I ask musicians to play or sing something specific. I may invite a congregation member, or even someone from outside the congregation, to preach. Often, I ask people who do good work with graphics and design to help with a handout. For one sermon on emotional triangles and conflict, a parishioner did a four-page booklet with amazing graphics that illustrated the key points. Members of the congregation are generally excited to help when asked. Part of the blessing of the sermon series is planning far enough in advance to utilize their enthusiasm.

Most sermon series look at the long-term focus from different angles. My first sermon in a series often covers the theological rationale. I sum up the strongest case for why the transformation is an essential part of following Jesus. The second sermon contains the practical vision. Building on the rest of the long-term sermon, I paint the picture of where we are today and where God is calling us to be. A key component of living into the next stage of that vision is learning and employing new behaviors that will move the congregation forward. I focus one or more sermons on how to move forward. Explaining how to engage the new behaviors is the key component of a sermon series. When people know they are focusing on something that the preacher thinks is particularly important, they are willing to be a little more uncomfortable. They know we are focusing on something new, so being pushed out of their comfort zone is not such a shock. Depending on what we are learning, I might ask the congregation to write things down, to think about things, to talk to their neighbor, or to do some sort of physical movement. Twice, I have created a series of hand and arm gestures to go with a sermon series that helped the congregation remember my points.

I also generally try to create handouts for my sermon series. Sometimes, the handout is a list of key points in the bulletin, especially for the early sermons. For the practical teachings, I usually have a handout where people can write down their answers to questions or complete exercises. Compiling some sort of booklet after the sermon series can extend its reach. In some cases, I have published sermon manuscripts for the entire series in a booklet and mailed them to the congregation, which reinforced the series for those who heard it and reached those who were not present. I have also created booklets of key components of the learning or practical exercises that were used in other contexts.

I have used series repeatedly to drive home elements of my long-term sermons. Usually, they come after the foundation has prepared the congregation to learn and apply a practical set of skills. When the long-term sermon is part of a broader congregational focus, the sermon series may follow a few months of groundwork for a variety of new parish initiatives. In those cases where I have discerned and chosen the focus myself, the sermon series is the capstone of an extended sermon before turning to the next stage of the congregation's journey of faith.

During an extended sermon about welcoming and evangelism, I chose the four weeks of Advent for a series. Week one focused on "God-sightings"—if people did not recognize where God was at work in their lives, they could not share that message with others. Everyone was given a card to write down where they saw God in the world around them, where they saw God in their own life, and a God-sighting they wanted to share with others. We ended the sermon with people sharing their God-sighting with someone else in the congregation.

The second week of the series involved the "Welcome, Engage, Connect" sermon I described earlier. The third week asked people to invite those in their network of family and friends who did not regularly attend a church. We handed out a card to help everyone think through their social networks and gave them a prayer card that they could return so the parish could pray for the people they wanted to invite. We also had a note card that said, "Counting my blessings . . . thinking of you" on the cover. I encouraged everyone to think about how they have seen someone as a blessing, and then write them a note describing how. Finally, we asked people to check off a volunteer card if they were willing to help with specific jobs supporting those inviting new people or guests who came. The gospel reading for the fourth week was the story of the visitation of Mary and Elizabeth. Given the practical work we had just done, the sermon focused on the theological rationale found in the deep hospitality that Mary and Elizabeth showed each other. Then we reviewed the steps we had just taken.

I have used other sermons series in similar ways. At the beginning of chapter two, I reviewed how I used a sermon series as the culmination of an extended stewardship-focused sermon. The example above about emotional triangles was part of a series on dealing with conflict. Others sermons in that series included an in-depth look at Matthew 18:15–20 and the introduction of a vestry-approved church conflict resolution process; a sermon on resentments; and a sermon on constructive dialogue with people who are different (which was based on a diocesan diversity training some of us had attended). At another time in our parish life, the congregation entered a process to understand our church's identity.

I preached through our new purpose statement, guiding principles, and strategic directions. In all of these cases, I believe the sermon series helped the congregation move forward.

The follow-up to a sermon series varies. Primarily, the follow-up takes place in contexts outside of the pulpit, since the practical skills learned need to be put into practice. Ideally, the sermon series is effectively coordinated with other parish activities to incorporate the congregation's focus and enthusiasm. Future sermons will generally supplement what is going on in the congregation as a whole. If the long-term focus continues, a preacher will probably be able to find multiple examples in the parish where the focus is being lived out. These cases can be incorporated in sermons and announcements on a regular basis to remind people of what they have learned and inspire them to continue.

Questions for Reflection and Discussion

- What subject in this chapter was most helpful in thinking about your own preaching?
- What practical skills, if any, have you taught during a sermon?
- Can you identify a time where not understanding how to engage in particular discipleship practices prevented your congregation from moving forward?
- How might your congregation be different if congregational activity was frequently highlighted in preaching and parishioners were asked to participate in the sermon?
- What parishioner gifts could you regularly include in your preaching?

Practical Exercises

- Outline a sermon series. The outline should include relevant scripture passages, sermon points, practical exercises, and draft handouts.

— 5 —

Discerning the Next Stage

Then the Israelites set out by stages from the wilderness of Sinai.
—Numbers 10:12a

WHEN I ACCEPTED my current call ten years ago, the first area of concern for the parish was stewardship. After focusing my preaching on that topic for a season, we needed to figure out where we were and where we needed to go. The church had a solid choir, a thriving Sunday school, a revitalized food pantry, and a dynamic women's group. They had also recently torn down a ninety-year-old gymnasium with a swimming pool that had not been used in years and replaced it with a new social hall and commercial kitchen. Opportunities existed for growth and development even in our Rust Belt community that had lost 40 percent of its population. We just needed to know where we were going.

Figuring out the next stage of our congregational journey was not straightforward. At their core, parishioners knew why their ministries were important. On the surface, however, most people carried out their work with great dedication and little understanding of how they fit into the larger picture. They loved their church and had been told at some point that working with children or feeding the hungry were important ways to live out their faith, so they did. Unfortunately, some ways of being church that had seemed effective for a few decades were no longer so. Without a clearer sense of direction, it was difficult to make changes in the church to respond to changes in the world.

A primary job of a pastor who is in the pulpit almost every week is to provide the parish a sense of direction. Somebody has to keep standing up and telling the congregation where they are going and offer suggestions for how to get there. A long-term sermon is one way that a preacher can lead a church through the wilderness to get one stage closer to the promised land.

The model of the Israelites traveling in stages through the wilderness is helpful for pastors. I would very much like to preach the one perfect sermon, get everyone saved and sanctified, and then sit down and let the choir take over. Preaching that transforms congregations does not work like that, however. Good preaching provides the tools a church needs for its current place in the wilderness. If we are at the foot of a mountain, some instruction about belays and carabiners is probably helpful, along with ongoing encouragement to stay roped together and not look down. If we have to cross a river, people in the pews either need to learn the backstroke or how to pray to part the waters. On the other hand, a desert-stage sermon on conserving water while staying hydrated is not going to be effective if everyone is knee-deep in frigid spring runoff. Nor can we really expect to tell people in a single sermon how to maintain a breath rhythm while they swim and expect them to be experts at it the following Sunday. Helping a congregation move toward the promised land takes continued intentionality and focus appropriate for each successive stage of the journey.

Of great importance, then, is figuring out what is important enough to focus on for the next year or two. For most pastoral-sized or smaller churches, a decision is necessary. Unless a church is large enough to have multiple cells ministering in different ways or has a steady stream of new faces, the congregation is probably only able to focus on one thing at a time. People who have been in the congregation for a while are usually already involved in the small groups and ministries that feed them. The number of people with extra time on their hands is generally limited, and often restricted to recent retirees, the widowed, or new empty nesters. Even dedicated congregants who want to grow their church and become more faithful disciples have limited bandwidth for new ideas and projects.

By focusing on one thing over an extended period of time, the preacher is able to catch people when they have extra time or energy in their own lives. Some people have additional flexibility when they reset their children's commitments as school starts in September. Others are happy to reengage when they return from their southern winters in the spring or their northern summers in late fall. Accountants in the parish are paying a lot more attention to sermons on April 20th than on April 10th.

Another goal of the long-term sermon is to allow the important teaching about the current stage of the church's journey to seep into the existing groups and ministries. Recognizing that most of the church is already engaged in good ministry, the goal is to increase the spiritual health and vitality of what the church is already doing, rather than add on an array of programming. If the needed focus is evangelism, ideally people in the food pantry will have conversations with each other about how their work helps spread the gospel. The choir may all decide to reach out to unchurched tenor friends to invite them to come sing so that they have a chance to learn about God through the liturgy while adding another voice. All the choir members leaving rehearsal to hand out welcome cards door-to-door is unlikely to be helpful, however. If the congregation's focus is loving relationships, the choir may realize that they have to focus on being more encouraging and supportive of one another before they start reaching out to others. While any number of programmatic plans and ministry evaluations can support the church's focus, a preacher consistently and generously proclaiming the good news about the congregation's greatest current need can provide the spark that moves individuals and ministries in the right direction.

This focus of about eighteen months to increase a church's health is often the form that interim ministry takes. After a long-term pastor leaves, the church or its judicatory may decide that before the next phase of its life the congregation needs to work on a specific area. Rather than immediately calling a new pastor, they may seek an interim with skills in their area of relative weakness. That interim can undertake the parish's general pastoral work while paying close attention to one area. The congregation would expect to hear sermons regularly that touch upon that area, and then apply those teachings throughout their congregational life. At the end of a year or two, the church will have moved to another stage in their journey, and the interim can move on.

In the same way an interim pastor helps a congregation through one stage of a journey, long-term pastors can think of their ministry as working through a series of stages. Discerning what stage the congregation is in and where it needs to go next are important questions.

In my current call, figuring out the focus of the next extended sermon has happened in a variety of ways. How closely that focus dovetailed with other congregational activity has also varied. Ideally, our next direction came about as a result of an intentional process of discernment and planning by the whole parish. Sometimes, however, the decision has been driven primarily by me, or primarily by the parish, or primarily by outside events. For us, the outside events that became at least a partial focus have included the opportunity to complete needed building improvements by joining the diocese in a capital campaign and by doing our own antiracism work in response to issues in the larger community.

When I first arrived, the vestry told me the focus had to be stewardship, so I went with it. After the congregation's stewardship increased, I had to figure out what was next. During our focus on stewardship, I began to learn more about both the parish history and to meet people in the community. I learned that St. John's had a long history of being a significant part of its city. In 1928, when Sharon, Pennsylvania, needed a place for children to learn to swim, the church built a swimming pool and gymnasium. During World War II, the parish opened its facilities to GIs about to ship out to Europe from neighboring Camp Reynolds. The church had always been a key player in founding local social service organizations, and even helped settle a bitter Westinghouse strike. Current community leaders did not feel connected to the parish, however. During construction of the new social hall, groups that met at the church had to find new homes and then did not return after it was completed. I believed the key to the parish's growth and development, as well as a central aspect of its call, was engaging the community around us.

I chose community engagement as the focus because that seemed to be the place that offered the maximum leverage to move the church closer to who God was calling us to be. Ideally, a pastor chooses an area of focus that has the greatest potential to transform a congregation. Anytime we pick a theme and stick with it, we have a chance to help move a church forward. Finding where the parish is stuck at a particular moment offers the best chance for leading the church into the next phase of its journey.

The point of maximum leverage for church health and growth is usually the church's current weakest area. When we ask ourselves what is most missing in the church, the answer often points us in the right direction. Is the congregation afraid of evangelism, or ignorant of how to do it? Do they love Sunday morning worship, but neglect Monday evening devotions? Do most meetings end in unresolved conflict, or does the rumor mill run twice as quickly as the prayer chain? Do visitors get lost trying to find the service time online or find an outside door locked when they arrive? Are people using their spiritual gifts in ministry, or signing up wherever their guilt has led them?

One process designed to increase church health and growth, called Natural Church Development, names this area of maximum leverage the church's "minimum factor."[1] All churches, no matter how healthy

---

1. Christian A. Schwartz, *Color Your World with Natural Church Development: Experiencing All That God Has Designed You to Be* (St. Charles, IL: ChurchSmart Resources, 2005), 124–29.

or how struggling, have a minimum factor. One of the images Natural Church Development uses for a church is a wooden barrel made up of vertical staves around the outside. Each stave represents a different area of the church's common life. A barrel can only hold as much water as its lowest stave and the church can only grow to the level of its minimum factor. As a congregation's minimum factor is improved, the church is able to reach and disciple more people.[2]

The tricky part of determining a congregation's minimum factor is that we, as pastors, might not see it. Sometimes the minimum factor of a particular congregation is also a weakness for a denomination as a whole, or for the individual preacher. Both clergy and laity often have blinders to their vulnerabilities, which is how they become weaknesses; instead, we focus disproportionately on areas of perceived strength. While increasing strengths can be important, they may not provide much forward movement for the church. To give one overly generalized example, historically Episcopal clergy have been trained to focus on the liturgy more than evangelism. When attendance began to decline, they sought a remedy by tweaking the liturgical language and the musical offerings in an already inspiring worship service. Because we lacked training in evangelism techniques, we ignored it as unfamiliar. The issue, though, was how to get people in the door, not offering them something meaningful when they got there. Conversely, a church that is great at evangelism may bring new people through the door in droves every Sunday but watch them leave just as quickly due to disorganized follow-up, systemic conflict, or an inadequate facility. Every church has a minimum factor, but that minimum factor is different for each stage of each church's journey. There is no one-size-fits-all answer to church development.

If a pastor has been in a church for a while, the congregation's minimum factor may mirror the pastor's weakness. To effectively preach and lead, the pastor will have to focus on their own growth, as well as the congregation's; to address that topic in a long-term sermon, preachers

---

2. Schwarz, *Color Your World*, 130–31.

need to do their homework, which might include some reading, time spent in prayer, and developing new practices.

Processes to Aid Discernment of Long-Term Preaching Focus

A preacher does not usually need to figure out a congregation's minimum factor on their own. A variety of processes and consultants can help a pastor and a church look at their common life and decide what areas provide the most helpful future focus. I am going to talk about four here, two of which I have used and two of which I can recommend because I have seen others use them. One of the strengths of all of these processes is the use of an outside coach or consultant to walk a pastor and a congregation through the process and keep them on track going forward. I have found such coaching exceedingly helpful in my own ministry, both for general ministry and for specific processes and purposes.

At St. John's, while I was preaching about engaging the greater community, I was also aware that the questions about parish identity and purpose remained unanswered. While stewardship and looking outward were both essential, we were not going to get very far without delving deeper into who we were and why we were here. In my search for answers to those questions, I came across a consultant named Dave Daubert, who now runs Day 8 Strategies.[3] His *Seeing Through New Eyes* was the perfect fit for what our congregation needed.

The underlying principles in Daubert's work were three simple yet compelling statements: "Be who you are; see what you have; do what matters."[4] For more than a year, Daubert helped us look at ourselves, our history, and our neighbors. We named assets and strengths and determined needs. We answered faith questions in journals, drew pictures, interviewed people on the street, and shared our hopes for the

---

3. For more information, go to https://www.day8strategies.com/.
4. A Renewal Enterprise, Inc., *Seeing Through New Eyes: Using the PAWN Process in Faith-Based Groups* (Chicago: A Renewal Enterprise, Inc., 2010), 11.

future. Daubert and his associate facilitated parish meetings, coached a leadership team, encouraged and challenged us, and helped us pull the information together into a final product to move us forward. When we were finished, we had created a parish purpose statement summarizing why we believe God created our church. We also had six guiding principles that describe who we are when we are at our best and five strategic directions where we felt God was calling us to move into mission and ministry. Of equal importance, we had brought people together across different ministries and small groups who were now invested in a common direction. The next phase of my preaching focus was to look at our purpose statement, guiding principles, and strategic directions.

Perhaps the most important result of defining ourselves through this process was that we could be encouraging and positive as groups and individuals took risks to live more fully into who we were called to be. We had a way to determine if proposals were in line with who we were; if they were, our default position was to approve and support the suggestions. This open attitude led to new ministries and partnerships almost immediately. The reinforcement through regular preaching was important, however, to overwrite old habits and reflexes with our new understanding of ourselves. No one was really opposed, yet we all knew of great ideas that sat in binders on shelves. My role in this process was to preach a long-term sermon that reinforced our identity, showed how our goals worked in different contexts, continually connected these new directions with God's call, and celebrated the places in the parish where this work was occurring. The long-term sermon was reinforced liturgically by a colleague who set our purpose statement to music we sang in response to the offertory sentence. Once our new understandings of our core identity and direction had taken root throughout the congregation, we began the work of crafting a long-term focus for the next stage.

The direction we turned to next was the Natural Church Development (NCD) process. Natural Church Development is an international ministry that has worked with tens of thousands of churches in over seventy countries. Participating churches range from Orthodox to evangelical to mainline Protestant to charismatic to underground congregations in countries where Christians are persecuted. NCD focuses on helping congregations develop into healthier churches because, their research shows, healthier churches grow.

NCD is an open process that allows for variation depending on the needs of the individual church. NCD's resources focus on organic principles found in both scripture and nature. These principles, which include interdependence, multiplication, and sustainability, help a congregation cooperate with God's work within it.[5]

The core of the NCD process is a congregational survey of thirty leaders who are involved in some type of small group. This scientifically scaled instrument looks at eight different areas of church life to identify the congregation's minimum factor: empowering leadership, gift-based ministry, passionate spirituality, effective structures, inspiring worship service, holistic small groups, need-oriented evangelism, and loving relationships.[6] Part of the beauty of NCD is an ecumenical assumption that these characteristics will look different in different churches. Depending on context, worship could inspire with billowing clouds of incense, a praise band, or the entire congregation praying in tongues. In one place, an effective structure might include a church mobile app, while in another everyone knows they can call the secretary to get the information they need. How things work is not as important as *that* they work.

The results of the survey enable the congregation to dig more deeply into its area of current weakness, make a plan to address that weakness, implement the plan, and then evaluate and start the process again. NCD recommends using a trained coach to lead a congregation through the process, and it trains and licenses coaches, allowing them to integrate NCD coaching into their own ministries. NCD has some resources to

---

5. Schwarz, *Color Your World*, 89–103.
6. Schwarz, *Color Your World*, 104–31.

address various minimum factors, but the process assumes that a church will draw from a wide variety of sources as it plans its next steps.[7]

I have worked through a number of NCD processes. The first cycle at St. John's found that our minimum factor was passionate spirituality. In chapter one, I described some of the ways I addressed this minimum factor in a long-term sermon. After focusing on spirituality, the next time we did an NCD survey our minimum factor was loving relationships.

Another process with some similarities to Natural Church Development is the Congregational Assessment Tool (CAT) from Holy Cow! Consulting. The CAT is a congregation-wide survey that provides a comprehensive look at the attitudes and behaviors of a church. It is an intensive process that involves significant congregational preparation before the survey and follow-up afterward. The results are processed either with a trained consultant onsite or through a video conference.

The CAT looks closely at eight areas of congregation life: hospitality, morale, conflict management, governance, spiritual vitality, readiness for ministry, engagement for education, and worship and music. Additionally, the CAT places the congregation in one of four quadrants based on the church's energy and satisfaction. Survey questions do a good job digging into the specific drivers of both energy and satisfaction. Parish priorities are discussed, and those priorities and other information are broken out by age and other demographic criteria that are helpful for the congregation. Demographic, attendance, and financial data are included components of the survey. The CAT also allows the church to customize questions important in its own ministry context.

Specific modules are available as part of the CAT survey to tailor the information more closely to the needs of the specific congregation, including questions for churches undergoing a pastoral transition, considering

---

7. For more information about Natural Church Development in the United States, contact NCD America, 4145 E. Campus Circle Drive, Berrien Springs, MI 49104, 1-888-836-7623, www.ncdamerica.org.

a capital campaign, working on a merger with another congregation, preparing for a stewardship appeal, developing better communication strategies, and facing a variety of other situations. The *Vital Signs* report generated by the CAT offers significant data for congregational discussion and future focus. Congregations receive an in-depth look at themselves at a key time in their life. A preacher can use the results, with the help of a consultant and congregation leadership, to focus a long-term sermon in conjunction with a parish-wide effort for maximum leverage. The CAT report may also provide enough data for a second focus once the initial area of work has been completed.

Holy Cow! Consulting also offers a less elaborate option called *Conversations* for small congregations with an average Sunday attendance under 35. They also have survey resources available for church boards, church staffs, and a *Family Tree* instrument designed to map out the relationships within a congregation.[8]

The fourth tool to assist in discerning how to preach in current stage of the congregation's life is RenewalWorks,[9] which is a tool that specifically focuses on spiritual growth and vitality. Based on research from two hundred Episcopal congregations and nearly twelve thousand parishioners, it offers churches a Spiritual Life Inventory (SLI) that helps congregations place themselves along a spiritual continuum from exploring a life with God in Christ, to growing that life, to deepening that life, to being centered in a life with God in Christ.

Following the SLI, RenewalWorks supports a congregational workshop team through a four-step process: *Where have we been? Where are we now? Where do we feel called to go?* and *How do we get there?* The goal is to help the church make a culture shift toward spiritual growth. RenewalWorks's strength is its spiritual vitality process tailored to the needs of Episcopal congregations, many of whom have spiritual vitality

---

8 For more information, go to https://holycowconsulting.com.

9. For more information, go to http://renewalworks.org/.

as a minimum factor in their church life. This focus makes it a perfect tool for some congregations and a less robust tool for those currently hamstrung in other areas.

Regardless of the process used to determine the focus of a long-term sermon, selecting and maintaining a focus will bear fruit. Preachers need to find a process that they are comfortable with for analyzing their congregation, since they will need to conduct such analyses multiple times. Each time a long-term sermon successfully leads to congregational transformation, a new focus will need to be discerned.

Questions for Reflection and Discussion

- What in this chapter made you think differently about how to determine a focus for your preaching?
- Does thinking about a series of long-term sermons as a succession of interim efforts to move a congregation make the idea more or less appealing to you? Why?
- What processes have you used in the past to discern a congregational development or long-term sermon focus?
- What kind of discernment process do you think would be most helpful for you to identify an appropriate focus for your congregation at this time?
- Some preachers have advocated preaching with the Bible in one hand and a newspaper in the other. Compare and contrast that approach with one that pays particular attention to congregational survey results as well.
- Have you ever preached or heard sermons on a congregation's mission statement? What seemed to work and what didn't in those sermons?

Practical Exercises

- Research at least two of the processes suggested for discerning a long-term sermon focus. What do you feel would be the strengths and weaknesses of each for your congregation?
- Write a sentence describing what you think your congregation's current minimum factor is. Share that sentence with your board or other key leaders and get their feedback.

– 6 –

Long-Term Sermon
Templates

Spiritual Gifts and
The Way of Love

*Do not, therefore, abandon that confidence of yours; it brings a
great reward. For you need endurance, so that when you have
done the will of God, you may receive what was promised.*

—Hebrews 10:35–36

FOCUSING ON A long-term sermon does indeed require endurance. So
often, preaching is easier if we can just move on to the next gospel passage,
the country's moral crisis of the week, or the shiny new idea that will save
the church. Of course, we do have to explicate the next gospel passage,
help the congregation see the news through a Christian lens, and take
advantage of the latest research and wisdom. We also have to find ways
to go deeper into what our congregation needs to hear at this moment

in their life, which means we need to go deeper ourselves. Rather than sprinting from Sunday to Sunday, we must develop the endurance of a marathoner that keeps taking the next step without abandoning our initial confidence, until we and our churches reach God's promised reward.

This chapter will flesh out two examples of what a long-term sermon might look like that teaches a congregation why and how to take the next steps toward growth and transformation. Each of these examples can be easily adapted for preaching an extended sermon in various contexts. My two foci in these examples are spiritual gifts development and *The Way of Love*. A long-term sermon based on either provides a foundation for the future redevelopment of a congregation.

Example 1: Spiritual Gifts Development

Spiritual gifts identification, development, and utilization can be the starting point for many different future emphases. Starting a multicycle process of congregational health and growth with an extended sermon focus on the development of spiritual gifts is useful for many reasons. As we talked about, we, as congregational leaders, often do not emphasize those areas where we and our denominations are traditionally weakest. Just because we have underemphasized an aspect of our church life does not mean that God has not provided the gifts we need in that area, however. A focus on spiritual gifts can help us identify and empower those in our congregations who have strengths where we have weaknesses. Identifying them can be the first step in further congregational health and development.

Beyond our weaknesses, a congregation is going to grow best when everyone is using the gifts God has given them to build up the body of Christ. When we place people in ministries that do not match their gifts, we put barriers in our own way. Business authors such as Jim Collins recognize the importance of this proper deployment. Collins's research into what makes a great company shows that as an early step in the process of development, the corporation must find the right people and then get them working on the right projects. He calls it "putting people in the right seats on the bus."[1]

In a church context, we have to assume that God is doing one of three things to ensure that we have the right people: either we already have the right people, the people we have will become the right people as we grow together in discipleship, or God will send us whoever else we need for the work we are called to do. We trust that if we are doing our work of evangelism, prayer, and ongoing formation, God will take care of recruitment and development. What we in the church need to focus on is getting the people we have in the right seats.

The work of spiritual gifts identification, development, and utilization is the process of putting people in the right seats. Without this step, many other congregational development initiatives will fall flat. A growing parish formation program will not thrive if the teachers are loving, long-time volunteers who do not have the gift of teaching, or if the leaders trying to move the program to the next level are lousy organizers. Worship will be less inspiring than it could be if those with strong gifts for music or artistic creativity are not involved in the liturgical planning process. Initiatives to reach new people in the community may fail because those with the gift of evangelism are too busy going to church committee meetings to focus on building relationships with people who are unchurched or de-churched. Most troubling of all, ministries may have no idea what spiritual gifts are needed for their work and may try to survive by guilting well-meaning people to continue to do what has always been done.

When parishioners know their spiritual gifts and know how to use them, the congregation has an easier path forward regardless of the direction God is calling them. Church leadership will be able to identify and appoint the people God has gifted for the work. When a congregation knows its members' spiritual gifts, change can also go more

---

1. Jim Collins, *Good to Great: Why Some Companies Make the Leap . . . And Others Don't* (New York: HarperBusiness, 2001), 57–58.

smoothly. Instead of prodding the entire congregation to take small, difficult steps, a smaller number of the people with the right gifts can take a significant step forward. Since those people have the appropriate gifts to the task, even that new, larger step will be much easier, and often more fun and rewarding.

Focusing on spiritual gifts development can be helpful if you have discerned that matching ministries with spiritual gifts is a current church weakness. It is also worthwhile if the congregation needs to make some changes but is unclear where to start. Working on spiritual gifts is a natural starting point for whatever the next steps might be.

A long-term sermon on spiritual gifts can be divided into five different areas. While some aspects, such as the theological rationale, are helpful to talk about early, the order can be adapted to the congregational context. Since a long-term sermon works by gradually introducing concepts to be heard, appropriated, and applied over time, the continual saturation of the focus is more important than the exact order of its aspects.

The five areas to incorporate into a long-term sermon on spiritual gifts are the theological understanding of spiritual gifts and the call to use them; a practical vision of what the congregation and the wider church would look like if we took gift usage more seriously; a concrete explanation of how spiritual gifts work in practice; an explanation of how to discover a person's spiritual gifts; and the explanation of particular spiritual gifts. These five areas draw on scripture and congregational examples in different ways. An extended sermon on spiritual gifts may also utilize a sermon series along the way to reinforce and reinvigorate congregational action.

One of the best resources I have found regarding spiritual gifts is *The 3 Colors of Ministry* by Christian Schwartz.[2] This Natural Church Development resource includes a good theological and practical

---

2. Christian A. Schwartz, *The 3 Colors of Ministry: A Ttrinitarian Approach to Identifying and Developing Your Spiritual Gifts* (St. Charles, IL: ChurchSmart Resources, 2001).

understanding of spiritual gifts, a very thorough spiritual gifts discovery test, explanations of thirty different spiritual gifts, and practical exercises designed to help individuals develop and begin using their spiritual gifts more effectively. Like all such instruments, Schwartz's work has some idiosyncrasies, and the survey requires a bit more math than the average instrument. Part of its strength, however, is the book's accessibility, with short sections of text and lots of full-color photos and diagrams. Like all of Natural Church Development's resources, *The 3 Colors of Ministry* incorporates the best of multiple Christian traditions around spiritual gifts. Schwartz has also written short companion guides for utilizing *The 3 Colors of Ministry* in small groups, mentoring relationships, and as part of a churchwide focus on spiritual gifts discernment and development.[3]

1. Theological Rationale

The theological explanation given to the congregation about spiritual gifts is fairly straightforward. Most preachers have given a sermon on spiritual gifts using 1 Corinthians 12 or Ephesians 4, or as part of the celebration of Pentecost. Emphasizing spiritual gifts when these passages and holy days arise is one way to talk about how the Holy Spirit distributes different gifts to each person to build up the body of Christ. This core understanding that God has provided each of us with different gifts we are meant to use in ministry is implicit in numerous other scriptural passages. Taking a minute or two to notice how actors in various readings are (or are not) willing to use their gifts, or how complimentary gifts are being used to benefit God's people, can be effective. Pointing out the

---

3. These guides are: Christian A. Schwarz and Brigitte Berief-Schwarz, *How to Study The 3 Colors of Ministry in Your Small Group* (St. Charles, IL: ChurchSmart, 2001); Christoph Schalk, *How to Use The 3 Colors of Ministry in a Mentoring Relationship* (St. Charles, IL: ChurchSmart Resources, 2001); and Christoph Schalk and Jon Haley, *How to Implement The 3 Colors of Ministry in Your Church* (St. Charles, IL: ChurchSmart Resources, 2001).

gifts of people like Moses and Aaron, Martha and Mary, or even Cain and Abel can reinforce a spiritual gifts focus. Another great example comes from Acts 14, when Barnabas and Paul are mistaken for Zeus and Hermes. Paul's gift of preaching combines with Barnabas's gift of encouragement. Their evangelism work might not go as well if Barnabas demanded equal speaking time. Exodus 17 offers the example of Aaron and Hur, who are required to hold up Moses's arms in blessing while Joshua fights Amalek. Because each one uses their gifts, the Israelites are victorious. If Hur had asked to switch with Moses halfway through, or if Aaron had tried to lead the troops, the battle might not have been won.

2. Practical Vision

The second element is a practical vision. We want the congregation to understand why utilizing spiritual gifts can help them, as individuals and as a whole, to live into God's calling more effectively. In many ways, this vision flows easily from the theological rationale and is not a difficult case to make. When people are using their gifts, everything goes more smoothly. Practical examples can be easily found in the church, in society, or in many movies of individuals who were able to do great things by utilizing their gifts instead of trying to work outside of their gifting. Cases of groups that begin to organize by giftedness instead of ego or traditional roles are also readily available.

Three items in particular are worth highlighting when casting the practical vision of increased use of congregational spiritual gifts. First, if people begin to use their spiritual gifts, the congregation will probably initiate new ministries, some of which may stretch the congregation in positive ways. People with gifts of hospitality start inviting people to come for meals, including people who are different in some ways from the average parishioner. Those with gifts of healing might start praying for people during or after worship. Evangelists may start pushing the parish to reach out in new ways. All of these are good—and part of a vision of a growing, thriving parish. Remember, though, part of preaching a vision where such new ministries could help transform the congregation is helping people to feel secure in the midst of change.

A second area to address as part of a practical vision is a move from a guilt-based to a gift-based ministry recruitment and staffing system. This aspect of gifts-based ministry should be a great motivation to individuals involved, helping them recognize how fulfilling and effective church work can be when it aligns with the work God created them to do. Recounting an experience about a time when the preacher or a parishioner gave up something they felt they "should" do in order to spend more time on what they were called to do is a strong witness.

A third point to keep in mind as we lay out elements of a practical vision is how people already engaged in ministries may feel. Many people already exercise their gifts in ministry, even if they have never taken a spiritual gifts survey. Other people may have spent a long time toiling away at something unsuccessfully because they do not have the gifts for the work. If they were told the work was essential and no one else was willing to do it, they may have been faithfully serving God and the church as best they could. We may need to find ways to recognize and honor that work while pointing beyond it. This honoring may be in private conversation or other contexts than the pulpit, but taking the time to do so is important.

In my first parish, I did not think the Sunday school was getting much traction and I laid out a vision for recruiting those with strong gifts of teaching to develop it. The way I spoke about that vision did not make the current teachers feel very good, even though they agreed with what I wanted to do. I wish I had found ways to honor better their past work while pointing toward how they could more effectively use their gifts in ministry that benefitted the young people they cared about deeply.

3. Practical Explanation of How Spiritual Gifts Work

The most important message to reinforce is that everyone has spiritual gifts. The Holy Spirit has given every single Christian one or more gifts to build up the body of Christ. From that message flows many other points to preach. Gifts benefit from training and development. Having a gift is not a magic wand to walk in and make everything work. Someone with the gift of teaching will still benefit from learning pedagogical methods, working with mentor teachers, and spending significant time developing lesson plans. When that effort is put in, however, that individual's students are going to benefit greatly, as opposed to someone without the gift of teaching who might do the same work, but without the same results. When individuals are operating out of their spiritual gifts, they often have a higher level of fulfillment and satisfaction. To someone utilizing their gifts, everything may seem easy, even when they are doing hard work. Such feelings act as beacons for where our spiritual gifts lie and are blessings from God as we use them.

4. Practical Instructions for How to Discover and Utilize Spiritual Gifts

In addition to general information about what spiritual gifts are and how they work, the congregation needs to know the specific ways that the church will implement a strategy based on spiritual gifts. As much as any long-term sermon focus, spiritual gifts require a coordinated effort outside of Sunday morning worship. Ideally, a churchwide spiritual gifts discovery initiative will accompany the sermon. Smaller activities can still be effective, however. At the very least, the preacher should ensure that a spiritual gifts discernment tool is available to the congregation. If no other avenues are offered in the parish, the preacher can set aside some convenient times for individuals or a group to learn more about their own spiritual gifts and how to use them. As in all church endeavors, the more people participate throughout the congregation, the more likely the spiritual gifts focus will lead to transformation. Sometimes, however, taking intentional small steps can help the flywheel of change begin to spin.

In addition to instruction about gifts surveys, discussing how to match up gifts and ministries is beneficial. Address the topic from both the perspective of ministries and the perspective of individuals looking for ministry opportunities. Just raising the issue in a thoughtful way can help ministry leaders as they think about their ministry and where it can go. Even if no one initially develops ministry descriptions that include spiritual gifts alongside duties and commitments, thinking about how spiritual gifts and ministries go together can begin to improve the congregation's work. As individuals look for ways to use their gifts, they will ask questions that prod deeper thinking.

Senior pastors may also recognize ministry areas that are underdeveloped or ministry areas that sorely need particular gifts to thrive. The example of asking for help based on giftedness instead of looking for someone with two free hours every other Wednesday evening leads the congregation to think in a new direction. Such "help wanted" sermons or announcement ads may also bring forth unexpected people that God has gifted to build up the congregation's ministry, but who otherwise might have been overlooked.

5. Explaining Specific Spiritual Gifts

One of the advantages of a long-term sermon on spiritual gifts is the ease with which the focus can be incorporated frequently into the week's sermon. Scripture specifically lists numerous spiritual gifts, and many spiritual gifts inventories supplement those lists with other gifts that are implied. Each time one of those spiritual gifts is explained in some way, the overall focus is reinforced.

Covering a wide variety of gifts over time is usually not difficult. Since everyone has spiritual gifts, everyone in scripture does as well. Taking a minute in a sermon to note a Bible character's spiritual gifts and how they are using them is straightforward. Examples from the parish where people are using spiritual gifts are also easy to find. Congregational illustrations are especially useful when gifts are used in unexpected ways. A person on the parish dinner team who knows nothing about cooking, but whose gift of hospitality makes her the perfect person to welcome everyone at the door is an easy-to-understand example. The preacher might mention a Sunday school volunteer whose gifts of service mean that he is great at setting up the rooms and taking care of other details so the teachers can teach.

Depending on the congregation, some gifts may need particular explanations. In the Episcopal parishes I have served, every time we talk about spiritual gifts, people have questions about the gift of tongues. Similar questions have arisen around prophecy and discernment of spirits. Explaining these gifts from the pulpit, and giving examples of their use within my own tradition, was always important not only to help people understand the gift in question, but also to feel comfortable with the idea of spiritual gifts as a whole. It would have been a mistake to assume that my mainline congregation did not have people who had experiences with more charismatic gifts. Between those who were raised in charismatic churches and those who had been part of renewal movements or healing ministries, more people than I would have expected had experience with speaking in tongues, discernment, or words of knowledge. Recognizing their gifts, while explaining to others what they were and how they could be used in our church, was essential.

A Spiritual Gifts Sermon Series

A sermon series as part of a long-term sermon on spiritual gifts can be most helpful in one of two places, either at the beginning or halfway through the sermon focus. At the beginning, a series can cover the theological rationale and practical vision of spiritual gifts. It can also provide concrete direction on how to discover and utilize those gifts, which invites receptive individuals to begin the process. The sermon series may either coordinate with an effort in the parish to allow people to discern their spiritual gifts, or some aspect of that discernment may be included in the sermon itself. Gift discernment instruments could be distributed or simple ones could even be taken during the worship service. After this kick-off, the long-term sermon could unfold over time with teachings about specific spiritual gifts and how to incorporate spiritual gifts into ministry.

The other place a sermon series is likely to be helpful is about half-way through the extended sermon focus. Over three to nine months' worth of sermons, the preacher will have incorporated teachings about spiritual gifts from a variety of perspectives. A small group within the parish may have taken a spiritual gifts inventory and begun to work with the results, which a sermon can highlight. The sermon series comes at the time when the preacher feels the congregation is ready to take a larger step forward. Follow the same basic pattern as when the series comes at the beginning of the long-term sermon, but reinforce instead of intro-duce. Since some parishioners may already be working with spiritual gifts, they can be invited to share their stories. The conclusion of the series is still some practical way members of the congregation can learn more about their own spiritual gifts and how to utilize them in ministry in that particular church.

Example 2: *The Way of Love*

Another long-term sermon focus that can work in a variety of circum-stances is *The Way of Love* because it covers a large range of discipleship practices and can be approached from a variety of angles. Any congre-gation that needs to improve its discipleship can build on this focus in directions that are applicable to its context. For preachers, choosing *The Way of Love* offers a framework that can be filled in with teachings and examples over the course of a one- to two-year period.

The Way of Love is a set of practices that Presiding Bishop Michael Curry challenged the Episcopal Church to live into during its 79th General Convention in 2018. *The Way of Love* contains seven compo-nents that can form a rule of life for discipleship. These practices are *Turn,*

Learn, Pray, Worship, Bless, Go, and *Rest.* Since that General Convention, a wide variety of resources have been made available for individuals and congregations to deepen their walk of discipleship using *The Way of Love.*[4]

I want to highlight *The Way of Love* in this work focusing on long-term sermons because I believe that an extended sermon is the most valuable approach for a congregation wanting *The Way of Love* to become its lens for discipleship. With seven different areas to think about in addition to learning about a rule of life, *The Way of Love* is probably more like a new language to be learned than any of the other examples I have used. The average person in our pews needs the vocabulary of that language to be reinforced again and again if they are going to appropriate the concepts for themselves and then begin to live them out. While options exist for small groups to delve deeply into *The Way of Love,* an extended sermon is necessary for a congregation as a whole. Even a seven- or eight-week sequence on the seven areas of *The Way of Love* is unlikely to be remembered six months later without ongoing emphasis.

Since a wide variety of resources exist for teaching the individual components of *The Way of Love,* I will focus here on the overall arc of a long-term sermon with this focus. An effective extended sermon utilizing *The Way of Love* to move the congregation forward in their discipleship has four components: an explanatory introduction, a series of illustrative examples, instruction on individual appropriation, and ongoing reinforcement.

1. Explanatory Introduction

The first step in utilizing *The Way of Love* with a congregation is teaching it. Seven areas are more than fits on the fingers of one hand and these concepts are not taken from any single scripture passage. None of the concepts are difficult or unfamiliar, but taken together they are easy

---

4. Many of these resources can be found at https://www.episcopalchurch.org/way-of-love.

to forget, transpose, or substitute. The concepts cannot be introduced on their own and then easily pulled together, as a long-term focus on spiritual gifts might do. Instead, an extended sermon on *The Way of Love* requires a sermon series kick-off.

One of the first worthwhile elements in a sermon series introducing *The Way of Love* will be a mnemonic to help people remember its seven components. In my congregation, we developed a series of hand gestures that went with each one. *Turn* involved extending our arms with palms outstretched and then turning the palms inward. *Learn* had us bring our hands together and then open them like a book. For *Pray*, we put our hands together in prayer. For *Worship*, we stretched our arms up and out, hands raised in an *orans* position. *Bless* had us stretch our arms out, palms down, as if we were blessings someone. For *Go*, we extended our arms with palms facing in toward each other as if we were motioning people out. Then for *Rest*, we made a pillow with our hands and lay our heads on them. The congregation enjoyed the motions, and they were effective in helping people learn the seven components. Developing the motions well enough to teach them cemented the seven practices in the proper order in my own mind.

The second area that needs to be taught in an explanatory introduction of *The Way of Love* is the idea of a rule of life. Since the seven practices of *The Way of Love* fit together as a rule of life, the congregation needs to understand that framework before they dive into the details. The explanation covers not only what a rule of life is, but also how everybody has one, even if it is implicit. Helping people see what they already do as a rule of life is necessary to help them make changes to it later. Handouts that provide people tools and time to write down their current rule of life are constructive at this point; such an exercise could also be saved for the third stage of the extended sermon.

Finally, the introduction needs to cover the seven practices themselves. Depending on the readings and the other items to address week by week, these practices could be covered in a number of ways. In some cases, the scripture readings will correspond adequately to the practices being described and the explanation can be incorporated organically into the week's sermon. In other cases, you might preach a sermon on *The Way of Love* practices instead of the week's texts, citing relevant scriptural passages as part of the sermon. The practices might also act as a sermon introduction, a sermon addendum, or a five-minute initial announcement. The most important thing is not where *Turn, Learn, Pray, Worship, Bless, Go,* and *Rest* are introduced, but that they are explained and tied together in a consistent way for the congregation.

2. Illustrative Examples

Once you have introduced the seven practices of *The Way of Love*, the next phase of the long-term sermon is to keep reminding the congregation of what they are. The most effective way to incorporate this focus into the weekly sermon is by noting examples. Most Hebrew Bible narratives and gospel accounts will have someone engaged in *Turn, Learn, Pray, Worship, Bless, Go,* or *Rest*. In the instances where no one is exemplifying a practice of *The Way of Love*, the preacher can easily point out how much better things might have been if someone did. Sometimes *The Way of Love* aside is fleshed out in some detail. Often, however, just connecting the current sermon back to *The Way of Love* is enough to reinforce the seven practices so that they stick.

In addition to scripture, congregational examples can buttress the church's learning. If something happening in the congregation engages the same practice as the Bible text, highlight that situation. When announcements are made about various ministries, they can be intentionally phrased to move the congregation on *The Way of Love*. Thinking about the long-term sermon as stretching into the announcements and bulletin blurbs extends its reach. The more the congregation sees the preacher using *The Way of Love* as an overarching framework to think about ministry and discipleship, the more they will be able to use the same framework in their own lives.

One important consideration in illustrating *The Way of Love* is regularly finding examples for all seven practices. Most congregations will find numerous opportunities to talk about *Bless*, and probably *Prayer* and *Worship* as well. *Turn* may be harder, especially in churches that do not focus on conversion. The congregation will need examples from all areas, however, or they will not know how to incorporate a less prominent area into their own lives, and they may decide those areas are not as important.

3. Individual Appropriation

After the congregation is familiar *The Way of Love* and has seen enough examples of what it means in practice, they are ready to do the work of incorporating the categories of *The Way of Love* into their own explicit rule of life. Depending on the circumstances, this step could be done in a single sermon with follow-up in different settings or over two or three sermons.

The first preaching emphasis in this stage is to remind the congregation what a rule of life is and how it works. With this background, the congregation is then encouraged to write out their own rule of life. It is helpful to have a handout with directions as well as space for writing. Part of the instructions given in the sermon and on the page should walk individuals through the different areas that already form an implicit rule of life for them.

Once people have written down their rule of life, the next step is to ask them to look at their rule in terms of the seven practices of *The Way of Love*. Hopefully they can see which areas are strongest for them and which are weakest. Encourage them to pick one practice to work on over the next six months in an area of their own weakness.

Much of this is easier to do in a small group then with the whole congregation on Sunday morning. Providing time and space for this exercise in a sermon, however, will reach more people and provide an expectation that having a rule of life focused on *The Way of Love* is what happens in your church. Following up in smaller groups is helpful in addition to the sermon time.

4. Ongoing Reinforcement

Once the congregation, or some of the congregation, has begun to engage with *The Way of Love* in a personal way, the long-term sermon continues to highlight the seven practices and how they are used. Ongoing reinforcement will usually look like pulling examples from scripture and the congregation as occurred in the illustrative examples phase. This stage can include three other very helpful components, however.

The first component is personal testimonies of how people have found their faith, their ministry, and their lives bettered by explicitly examining their rule of life and making adjustments based on *The Way of Love*. Once people have seriously struggled with living into what they have learned, they can share those struggles and successes with the rest of the congregation. In some cases, those can be shared by the preacher but ideally, they are shared by individuals or by a person being interviewed by the preacher.

The second component is a practical refresher of how individuals can look at their own rule of life and make intentional changes. Some in the congregation will not look at their rules of life the first time around, either because they need more time or because they missed church the weeks that information was preached. The congregation, as a whole, probably does not want to hear all the instruction sermons preached again. Talking for a minute or two about how the rule of life works after someone has shared their experience flows naturally. The preacher can also remind the congregation every so often about where they can get more information on rules of life, where to find the handouts about examining their own rule of life, or when small groups might be meeting that support people as they make positive changes. The main idea is to ensure that everyone in the congregation knows how to take the next step when they are ready, and that anyone new who comes to the church can see this work as part of their commitment.

Finally, six months or a year after the individual appropriation phase, the preacher can invite the congregation to look at their rule of life again. Since *The Way of Love* is not meant to be static, once the congregation has made intentional changes to their rule of life, they also need to evaluate how those changes are going and make any necessary tweaks. This process of reevaluation is the last important piece of a long-term sermon focusing on *The Way of Love*. Once this step has been accomplished, the congregation is ready for the next long-term sermon focus.

Questions for Reflection and Discussion

- What did you learn in this chapter that helped you better understand a long-term sermon?
- How do the two extended sermon models differ from other work you have experienced around spiritual gifts or *The Way of Love*? What do you think the difference in results would be?
- What most excites you about maintaining a consistent sermon theme over an extended period? What most scares you?
- What techniques described in this or earlier chapters would be the biggest departures from your normal preaching style?

Practical Exercises

- Create an outline for a long-term sermon series on either spiritual gifts or *The Way of Love*. Include a timeline, scripture readings to use, congregational examples, parishioner gifts to incorporate, and handouts to distribute.

Part 2

Preaching with Prayer, Passion, Personality, and Physicality

– 7 –

Prayer

Let the words of my mouth and the mediation of my heart be
acceptable in your sight, O LORD, my strength and my redeemer.

—Psalm 19:14, *The Book of Common Prayer*

OF ALL THE DISCIPLINES necessary for effective preaching, none is as central as prayer. We as preachers have the call, and the sheer audacity, to stand up in front of God's people and share God's good news. We have been given time to say something amid beautiful music, passionate intercession, the baptism of new Christians, the celebration of the Eucharist, and the reading of scripture itself. This charge is profoundly humbling, and can only be undertaken responsibly by offering ourselves, our congregation, and time of proclamation to God. Every time we stand before the church, we rely on the Holy Spirit to show up mightily. As a colleague of mine says, "If the Holy Spirit doesn't show up, all I have are pretty words."

While nothing we can do will make the Holy Spirit materialize at the appropriate place in our sermon outline, we can remove barriers that keep the Holy Spirit out. I believe that God desperately longs to be in the midst of our worship and preaching, and the Holy Spirit will show up to the degree that we are willing. This encounter is what all our worship is meant to facilitate. In my preaching, I always hope that the members of the congregation have an experience of God. Sometimes what I say sparks a new way of thinking about God or engagement in a new practice. As people hear a long-term sermon, they may understand God and the church in a way that clarifies their communal call more deeply. Those outcomes can deepen people's relationship with God as they appropriate the sermon teaching and application going forward. Sometimes, though, God encounters people more directly in the sermon. They may be encouraged or convicted, feel a forgiveness or freedom from sin, shame, or tragedy, or otherwise come to experience the fruits of the Holy Spirit. In some cases, when people have these encounters, they can identify something in the sermon that launched them beyond the words. At other times, links to the sermon topic or the preaching itself are not discernable except for God's free presence and action alongside whatever holy work we as preachers are striving to do.

The first part of this book detailed a system for moving a congregation to a new stage of their common life through deliberate, intentional sermon planning and execution over a period of months or years. I have witnessed the effectiveness of implementing such a rational schema. The Holy Spirit works through our preparation and planning, and God often blesses such efforts when we make them. Nevertheless, the most logical and judicious sermon construction based on an accurate assessment of our congregation's needs will never be enough by itself to achieve what we hope will occur in our preaching. We need to preach our most well-discerned, technically competent, and emotionally moving sermons, but we need to preach them within the Holy Spirit's surprising, untamed, and astounding work. Even when we are deliberately moving the congregation toward the next stage of their journey with all our skill and wisdom, we know that only God is going to get them there.

To open our preaching to what is beyond our words, prayer is essential. I have found that incorporating three areas of prayer into my sermon preparation has proven extremely fruitful. These areas are praying for discernment about what I am supposed to preach, praying for those who are going to hear my preaching, and praying for the space in which the preaching will take place. While these may happen at different times and in different ways, when they occur I find the transformative experiences I hope for in the congregation happening in richer ways.

Praying for Discernment about the Sermon

Over a decade ago, I stumbled across a blog post by Bishop Dan Martins of the Diocese of Springfield. I often disagree with him, but sometimes find his writing thoughtful in a way that helps me clarify my own thinking. I was digging around for something he wrote about the controversy of the day when I found a post on preaching. He talked about how he is "devout to the point of superstition about beginning the process of preparing every sermon with conscious and intentional prayer."[1] Then he related a prayer he used as he began to prepare a sermon. I have adapted that prayer and use it regularly throughout my sermon preparation process, including as I prepare to move to wherever I will be preaching from. The prayer I say is, *Lord, let your gift flow one more time, for the glory of your name, for the welfare of your people, for the salvation of my soul. Let your gift flow one more time.*

This prayer summarizes what I hope happens in the midst of my preaching. First and foremost, I need God's gifts to be able to preach at all. Even basic elements in sermon preparation like discernment, creativity, and exegesis are lavish blessings that God gives to us for the building up of God's people. Simply figuring out something helpful to say among the wide variety of topics and directions presented in an average week's lectionary texts can be daunting. Add in all of my own issues, fears,

---

1. Daniel Martins, "Woe to Me If I Preach Not the Gospel," June 12, 2017, https://cariocaconfessions.blogspot.com/2007/06/woe-to-me-if-i-preach-not-gospel_12.html.

and recalcitrance, and I know that it is only by God's gift that I can deliver a sermon that profits anyone at all. I know, too, that God has enabled me to preach in ways that have touched hearts, brought people closer to God, and resulted in changed behaviors that have built up the church. My prayer is that God would provide those gifts again so that my preaching might achieve God's mighty purposes for it. My prayer is also for God's blessing on the specific sermon I am preparing. I am not asking to become a great preacher, or to be given God's gift for me to utilize in the future. I am yearning for God to be powerfully present for my congregation the next time I am called to stand before them. I will happily come back again begging for God to do the same thing next week.

I pray for three overarching effects of my sermon. The first is glory to God. I hope and pray everything I do, especially everything I do in ministry, gives glory to God. Getting up in front of a church and talking about God should, first and foremost, glorify God's name. I want everyone to understand that whatever they hear or experience as part of the sermon comes from God. I also want my human efforts to be the best use of my skills in ways the please God and become a fragrant offering.

Second, I pray for the welfare of God's people to increase through my preaching. Since I am taking the risk to stand up and proclaim a message of God's love and way of life, I want the congregation present to benefit. I hope with every fiber of my being that God will take what I am offering and use it in amazing ways with every person present, and then bear fruit in countless other lives through their ministry. I want nothing I do to be fruitless or, worse, to be harmful to the congregation.

Finally, I pray for the salvation of my soul. Honestly, this line was in Martins's prayer, and when I first prayed, it felt a bit dramatic. My salvation does not depend on the quality of my preaching—at least I hope not—yet the more I pray this line, the more I realize that since I have been called to be a preacher, the more fully I live into this call and allow God to work in me through the call, the closer I get to God. More importantly, using my call improperly would be damaging to my relationship with God. The ways that unhealthy ego, control, or neediness can creep into preaching are many. Sloth and arrogance that lead to lack of preparation are also temptations. The power that comes as an authority figure standing in front of the congregation has been the downfall to many preachers over time and has resulted in a great distrust of the church and its leaders. I pray that my work in preaching brings me more fully into the salvation of God instead of drawing others or myself away from it.

Beyond this specific prayer, my preparation for preaching has components of continual prayer and discernment. Much of this prayer is listening to where God would lead me as I do my work. If I am paying attention, I often find the Holy Spirit nudging me to the right preaching resources, the right time to work on the sermon, and the actual sermon points.

Like many preachers, my bookshelf is full of commentaries on scripture and other resources. Especially on familiar gospel passages, I have more relevant pages on my bookshelf then I can read in preparation for a single week's sermon, never mind the tools included in Bible software packages and online preaching websites. I have also found that the insights of certain commentators can excite me so much that I overlook other important aspects of the sermon focus. Just because a new concept is significant to me and my personal scriptural devotion does not mean the congregation needs to hear it. Praying to be led to resources I need for the sermon required that week usually results in being drawn in the right direction.

I also have a daily practice of centering prayer. Often the central idea for a sermon comes when I engage in silent prayer, either as part of my regular practice or because I just stop everything for a while and offer the time to God. I also am often led to the time when I am supposed to work on putting the sermon together. My experience is that just because I have decided I have time to write a sermon on a certain day does not mean that I can or should write it that day. On some occasions, I have tried to write anyway and then had to throw the sermon out and restart it later. I can set aside time for sermon research, as well as for prayer about the sermon, but for the sermon itself I have to trust

God's timing to bring it to birth. To the degree that I am anxious about getting the sermon done or unsure of what I am doing, once I have done my exegesis and study, the next step is to just make time and listen to God until I learn what I need to do next. Sometimes what I hear is, "Now isn't the time. Don't worry."

When the time is right to start writing or outlining the sermon, I continue to feel God's direction if I am prayerfully paying attention. Often as I am working out the text or bullet points, I feel a tug to move this way or that. The clearest pull is often a strong "no" in my mind about one idea or another. When I find that my fingers do not want to type something, I have learned the hard way that it is best to just put that idea aside. Sometimes another point needs to be inserted that I would have missed had I moved to the next section. I can stop and listen, and often find an important direction that I had not yet considered. Then I can continue with my other thoughts. Other times the idea I have is unhelpful in some way and needs to be left on the cutting room floor. On occasion, I have ignored those promptings in favor of my own good ideas; I have never had someone come up afterwards and say that part of the sermon spoke to them in a meaningful way.

I also try to pay attention to those kinds of nudges when I am actually preaching the sermon. I think most, if not all, preachers have had the experience of feeling like they need to say something they had not prepared. These "divine insertions" can be the pieces that are the most important for folks that day. One week, I felt the call to take an aside and explain why the Christian hope of resurrection is incompatible with séances and trying to get dead people to talk with us. One of my newer members came up afterwards to say that they had never thought about that issue before and had been invited by friends to a séance the next week but would now refuse that invitation.

Sometimes God nudges other people to get a sermon where it needs to go. One week when the gospel reading from the lectionary included Jesus comparing divorce and adultery, I focused my sermon on something else. I had preached a sermon about that gospel passage the last time it came up and did not want to preach it again. My wife noticed, however, that some of the divorced people in the congregation looked troubled after the gospel was read. At the end of my prepared sermon, she raised her hand and asked me to explain what Jesus meant. I had the opportunity to explain a difficult text that people in the congregation really needed to hear. I would not have done so, however, if I had not been open to following God's lead through her unforeseen question.

Praying for Those to Hear the Sermon

One of my most important sermon preparation practices is praying for the people who are going to hear my sermon. I want them to hear what they need to hear from God. When I am praying for my sermon preparation, I am praying that with God's help, I will say what those in the congregation need to hear from me. The core of my prayer for preaching, however, is really that the congregation hears from God, regardless of what I say or don't say. I recently preached at a joint Ash Wednesday service and the host pastor prayed for us all at the beginning of the service. Part of his prayer was that God's Word would be heard through me or in spite of me. As we were walking from his office to the back of the church, he pulled me aside to make sure I was not offended by what he had prayed. Of course, I wasn't. His prayer was spot on. Better that the people hear from God with a lousy sermon than that they miss what they are meant to hear with technically remarkable one.

As a rector in a fairly stable parish, I have a pretty good idea who I will be preaching to each week. Almost all the names of those in attendance are in our parish directory, especially if I add the names of our regular visitors, guests, and new members since the last directory was printed. These lists are not small, yet I take seriously the discipline of praying for them every day as their rector and as their preacher. I also make sure that I pray for them before I begin to do any work on my sermon. If I have time Monday morning for sermon research, I say the prayer I listed in the last section, then pull out my directory and pray for my people first. Then I start reading. I do the same thing before I start writing later in the week.

I also try to take some time during the week to pray intentionally for guests and visitors to be drawn to worship. Often that prayer takes the form of bathing the surrounding community with light and asking God to draw the people to church that need to experience God's love in a way that we are able to share it. I find that as I or others in the congregation pray for new people to join us, we have visitors and guests who come and are ministered to by the sermon, the liturgy, and our ministries.

These prayers for the congregation, either for those already part of the church or for those we hope will become part of the church, lay the foundation for their encounter with God in the sermon. We want people to look forward to what they will experience during worship, whether in the preaching, the music, the sacrament, the prayers, or some other aspect of what happens. People who expect to hear something from God are going to be more receptive to what God might want to say to them. I want to preach to people who are hungry to hear what God is saying, and I make the time to pray that will happen.

Those in the pews come to church eager to hear what God wants to say to them. In our contemporary society few social incentives exist for attending church beyond seeking a deeper faith and an encounter with the living God. While some might bewail the attendance declines since the days when everybody seemed to go to church, one benefit is that those who come really want to be there. Our prayers for those attending help to deepen their longing for God and an encounter with God's word. Our prayers for our preaching prepare us to provide them the word they long to hear.

Our prayers for our congregation have one other important effect. As we pray for people, we develop a deeper love for them. Our prayers connect us to one another and connect us together with God. As our love for them deepens through prayer, we will be increasingly concerned about their needs in our preaching instead of being driven by our own ego or fears. The more we pray, the more we overcome whatever barriers are in us to proclaim the Good News to those before us. Preaching can be a scary endeavor, especially when we make strong claims for the love and justice and mercy of God, but we know that love casts out fear. A deep abiding love for our people helps us continue to take the risk of proclaiming those messages week after week. Praying regularly for the congregation is the most sure and certain way to develop that love.

Praying for the Preaching Space

The last element of prayerful preparation for preaching is praying for the space itself. Once I have prayed for myself and my preparation and for the congregation, I want the area where the sermon will be heard to be bathed in prayer.

My experience is that I can feel God's presence more powerfully at work in those places into which God has been regularly invited, or even begged, to be present. Believers and nonbelievers both describe a sense of peace or of light in sacred places where numerous people have prayed. I may not be preaching in a site that has received pilgrims for the centuries, but I do want everyone who enters to feel God's presence and power.

Practically, praying for the space means that the night before I preach, I pray for the church to be filled with God's light. Even if I am not physically at the church, I lift up the sanctuary to God and see the light of God's presence filling it. This prayer often brings a feeling of pure joy as I anticipate the encounter I and the congregation will have in this holy space the following morning. Other times, the prayer is more difficult and feels like work. Especially in those times, beseeching God to fill the church with love and grace seems essential as I pray through whatever resistance is in me or the church. I try to repeat this prayer for God to fill the church before I preach by praying in the church before the service. Given the uncertainty of what may arise on Sunday morning before the service, I find the Saturday evening prayer essential just in case.

I also take time to pray periodically in the church for an extended period. Sometimes I will light the thurible and spend a half hour incensing all the areas in the church, going up and down every pew and aisle and praying for those who will be sitting there. About quarterly, either I or a group of colleagues and I will come together and pray that God will fill the space. Depending on what we feel God is calling us to do, we might anoint all the pews and the windows and doors with oil, or just sit in a circle and quietly pray. Whatever form the prayer takes, we want to continually offer the sanctuary to God and invite God to be at work in our midst there.

Any preaching requires the Holy Spirit to speak to the congregation if the sermon is going to bear fruit. Prayer is the most valuable gift we have for calling on God to show up in the midst of our preaching. If we want to see people enter more deeply into a life of God individually and as a congregation, we need to dedicate ourselves to prayer even while we labor on the technical craft of preaching. The most well-planned and executed long-term sermon weaving seamlessly through the weekly sermon will still fail if the Holy Spirit doesn't show up.

While I believe that the preacher is primarily responsible for the prayer described in this chapter, the congregation also has a role to play. If parish leaders or those with a call to pray hold the preacher, the congregation, and the space up to God, their prayers will bear fruit. Sometimes it is said that churches get the preacher they deserve. A church that is praying for its preacher is likely to be blessed with better preaching, and richer encounters with God during the sermon.

Questions for Reflection and Discussion

- What elements of this chapter made you think about the connection between prayer and preaching in a new way?
- Of the kinds of prayer described in this chapter, which ones feel most important for preaching to bear fruit?
- What have been your customary prayer practices in preparation for preaching? What new prayer disciplines are you interested in beginning?

■ What role do you think the prayers of the congregation have on preaching? How might the congregation be invited to take that role more seriously?

Practical Exercises

■ Spend a week engaging in some of the prayer practices described in this chapter that are not part of your normal routine in preparation for preaching. After the sermon, spend at least twenty minutes describing how the prayer felt and what difference, if any, you experienced as part of the sermon and the surrounding worship.

■ Make a list of emphases you would like prayed for as you prepare your preaching. Share that list with the leaders in your congregation and ask them to take responsibility for praying along with you.

— 8 —

Passion

Always be ready to make your defense to anyone who demands
from you an accounting for the hope that is in you.

—1 Peter 3:15b

DURING A HOMILETICS CLASS in seminary we were given the assignment to preach a three-minute sermon on the "hope that is within us." The task seemed easy enough—until I sat down to write. Then the difficulties mounted. What scripture do I pick? Where do I focus? Three minutes is too long to stand up and recite the last lines of the Nicene Creed ("We look for the resurrection of the dead, and the life of the world to come"), but too short to ramble through some eschatological discourse. Neither of those options made for a very interesting sermon, anyway. Deep down, what was the hope that I had appropriated out of the great Christian story and cleaved to so strongly that I was willing to give my life to it? I realized I didn't know.

I was raised Roman Catholic and came into the Episcopal Church after I married a Methodist. I had been involved in church all my life and had seen Christianity lived out in ways that made a difference in the world. I had focused on loving God through prayer, worship, and service to the church and on loving neighbor through an array of corporal and spiritual works of mercy. I knew what I was supposed to do to have a relationship with God and to live a moral life. While preparing for that class sermon, though, I realized I had never clarified for myself the true hope within me in a way I could articulate. I had an idea of what I needed to do but could not really say where I was going. I came up with something that completed the assignment, and then set out to answer the deeper question.

Not everyone starts preaching as unsure about the question as I was. Christians from different traditions or with different backgrounds are often compelled to give an account of the hope within them much earlier in life. I occasionally wonder how I made it to seminary before I faced the task. At some point, we all need to grasp the hope within us if we are going to preach the Good News compellingly. The hope that is in us provides our understanding of what the Good News of Jesus Christ looks like when it comes to us, our loved ones, our church, our community, and our world. Without an accounting of our hope, we will be hard pressed to offer a compelling vision.

The hope within us is not static, of course. As we grow and change, as we deepen our relationships with others, and as we experience God in different ways, the way we conceive of our hope matures. God never changes, but our understanding of our inmost longings for God does. These profound yearnings of our heart, refracted through the lens of faith, can shine forth as our inspiring vision. When we give ourselves and our preaching over to this deeply cultivated vision, we tap into our fiercest passion for the Good News—a passion that ultimately propels our preaching.

We have talked about the importance of a practical vision as part of preaching a long-term sermon. That same practical vision is essential for all of our preaching. Any sermon, including an extended sermon, will contain only a piece of my own vision. Without that piece, I am not sharing the good news God has given to me. I need a way to focus on that practical vision, which is my concrete sense of what the reign of God looks like.

One question I ask myself is, *After the resurrection on the last day, when the New Jerusalem comes down from heaven, what is going to be different around here?* It helps me think both expansively and concretely about aspects of life today that will be transformed. Instead of starting with life as it is, I try to imagine how things will be when God's will *is* done on earth as in heaven. The beauty and love in such a vision, and the accompanying healing and grace, are so powerful that I want to do the hard work facing today's difficulties in light of that hope.

Others may use different questions or conceptual models to provide the necessary spark for their preaching passion. Presiding Bishop Michael Curry, drawing from Verna Dozier, talks about the nightmare of our current reality contrasted with the dream of God. The Beloved Community is another overarching image that helps us think about where we want to be and also illuminates the path to getting there. Whatever method helps us get there, our best preaching is anchored in a vision of a reality that comes when all creation is reconciled to God and is walking in God's ways.

Preaching Pitfalls

Focusing on a vision stemming from our hope protects us from a variety of pitfalls. When we are not preaching out of our deepest passion for God, sermons can become exercises in entertainment or personal aggrandizement. More insidious, however, is when preaching disconnects from our vision in ways that may seem appropriate but fall short of proclaiming true good news.

One such pitfall is preaching focused on what the congregation is supposed to be doing. A vision of a church that has fewer problems than the one before us requires so much less prayer and imagination than a vision of the reign of God. We can picture a church that gives more money, repaints Sunday school classrooms, and is nicer to the preacher more easily than we can imagine the difficult person in the third row singing "Hosanna" in the heavenly choir stall next to us for all eternity.

This danger can even sneak into long-term sermons or other seemingly appropriate congregational development efforts. The church may indeed need to focus on evangelism, but that goal should stem from the Great Commission and the overwhelming joy of people's encounters with Jesus rather than a desperate need to see the budget balanced. A solid practical vision of our deepest hope inoculates us against this problematic tendency. When we know that our vision is too vast for us to accomplish on our own, our preaching will reflect both our hope of what God is going to do and our desire to respond appropriately.

Another preaching pitfall when we forget our passion is slipping solely into scriptural exegesis. When I pull out commentaries and other resources about a passage, I usually find out all sorts of amazing things. Books have been written about every lectionary passage, so finding fifteen minutes of historical context, issues in translation, archeological insights, or connections to other ancient literature is no problem. It seems that much, although certainly not all, of that knowledge might be interesting to my congregation. They might even think I am erudite and interesting if I share it well, but preaching is not just about illuminating and explaining what has been written. God also calls us to connect the scriptures to the good news of our hope in God and offer the congregation ways to respond. We cannot ignore scriptural study, but neither can we stop there.

Unfortunately, these and other pitfalls are all too easy to fall into. On more than one occasion I have written a sermon that was a great talk, not a passionate sermon. By passionate sermon, I do not necessarily mean a sermon with lots of pulpit pounding or emotional expression. I mean a sermon where I care about what I am saying so much that I want to do whatever I can to share that message with others and get them to respond. When the sermon does not spring from the passion that God has given me, I have found that I should not preach it. Ideally, as I review the sermon in preparation for Sunday morning, I will realize I need to change it. At that point, I pray and sift through what good news I am called to proclaim. Maybe I need to make a few tweaks, but sometimes I need to start over. A few times I have actually preached a sermon for our early service that did not tap into my deep hope for the congregation. On those days, which I try desperately to avoid, I have reworked the entire sermon between services. The revisions are less polished, but because they contain what I am truly convicted to say that morning the later sermon is much more effective.

In some cases, another set of eyes or ears can help us realize we are not tapping into our passion. As I have worked with newer preachers, I find that one common issue is a lack of trust in their own passion. Since most preachers have heard numerous sermons on familiar scriptural passages, we have in our minds a variety of points that seem like they should be included in a sermon. We can easily stuff a sermon with what we think is supposed to be said and ignore the passion God has given to us. Having someone tell us to cut the snippets of sermons past and expand where our passion would take us is a gift that we all need. We benefit greatly from colleagues that will trust our vision while helping us learn to trust it ourselves.

Preaching a Lifetime Sermon

More than just protecting us from preaching mistakes, preaching out of our vision provides the passion that drives us to stand up week after week and share the deepest longings of our heart with God's people. Preaching is difficult, scary work. Comedian Jerry Seinfeld has a bit about more people being afraid of public speaking than of dying. Even so, we are the ones who stand up at funerals and on Sunday mornings and many other days to share challenging, transformative truths about God's power and love. Our passion to share our vision of the reign of God and to see it realized keeps us turning on our microphones and opening our mouths. Especially when our prayers for our congregation have developed our love for them and attuned us to God's good news for them, we have to preach.

As we share this good news springing from our passion for the reign of God, we have the opportunity to transform individuals and congregations. Our preaching scope is no longer a single sermon, or even a long-term sermon, but a lifetime sermon as we preach different aspects of the vision that God has given us. Individual sermons have particular themes and touch people in specific ways. Over time, however, our passionate preaching of the hope deep within us will portray different aspects of the vision in ways that allow our church to see an entire canvass of God's salvation and love. Our passion for the hope that is within us to come to fruition is the north star that guides our preaching and our ministry.

Our vision of the reign of God needs to be comprehensive enough to encompass the breadth of our preaching. On the one hand, every significant section of scripture should contribute to that vision. Whatever passage we are preaching should correspond to aspects of our hope. Sometimes scripture will challenge us to expand our vision or amend it to better correspond with God's will for us. If we have prayed into our vision, however, the texts for the week will usually illuminate our hope for the congregation more vibrantly than we could ourselves.

On the other hand, the comprehensiveness of our vision of the reign of God should cover as much of the human condition as is within our experience. Our hope is in God, and we can find God acting throughout salvation history in many different ways with a reconciling love. At an individual level, our practical vision will recognize the healing, forgiveness, and liberation we all need in order to accept and experience God's unconditional love for us. At a family level, God's reign has to include reconciliation of even deeply broken relationships. At a church level, our hope will include the body of Christ made up of those from every tribe, language, people, and nation worshipping God. At the societal level, our vision of the reign of God must encompass a robust understanding of God's justice and righteousness for all people while allowing for the lifting up of the lowly and the poor being filled with good things. Preaching the Good News at different times and places will require us to develop a longing for God's reign in all of these areas, even if the details look slightly different for each of us based on our own experiences.

Our vision is what God is calling us to preach, even if we share different aspects of it at different times and places. Paul provides a useful model. He received a heavenly vision of God's reign directly from the resurrected Jesus. That vision came as he was healed from his own brokenness and forgiven of the significant sins he had committed. While we may not all be struck blind on the road, part of the passion that drives us to share the vision is the unconditional love God shows for us in our darkest and most difficult times. After Paul received the vision, he preached it. As he said to King Agrippa, "I was not disobedient to the heavenly vision" (Acts 26:19). Sometimes he preached the basic message of Jesus crucified, died, and risen, and sometimes he preached components of the core gospel or its implications in the lives of his communities. His preaching at the Areopagus (Acts 17) was not exactly the same as his message to the Corinthians about proper use of spiritual gifts (1 Cor. 12). In both situations, however, he shared an aspect of the Good News of Jesus Christ that forms the core of his hope.

We also are going to preach the heavenly vision we have received. Our passion for that vision is the plumb line that leads us deeper into proclaiming our most vivid hope and good news. Regardless of the sermon topic for the week, our passion is the guide that will allow us to find aspects of our vision of the reign of God that correspond to it and share those aspects with the congregation.

Motivating Bold Preaching

Our passion communicates from our hearts to the hearts of the congregation. Such passion is recognized as necessary even in secular contexts. In speaking about the challenges of any adaptive leadership, Ronald Heifetz and his coauthors instruct leaders to speak from their heart. "[I]nspiring people calls for you to *speak* from the heart. . . . If you care deeply about the challenges facing people, find a way to tell them. You need to be moved yourself at the same time you seek to move others."[1]

---

1. Ronald Heifetz, Alexander Grashow, and Marty Linsky, *The Practice of Adaptive Leadership: Tools and Tactics for Changing Your Organization and the World* (Boston, MA: Harvard Business School Press, 2009), 269.

Heifetz's words are good advice for preachers seeking to help their congregations undertake the adaptive change that living into the vision of
the reign of God requires. To inspire our congregations, we need to love
them enough to be moved ourselves as we preach to them.

When I preach out of the passion that I have for my congregation
and my vision of the reign of God, I am challenged to preach at the edge
of my comfort zone and beyond. Specifically, I am called to proclaim
the good news about God that is at the farthest frontier of my faith.
Nothing less than the boldest statements about the unconditional love
and continuing power of God acting in our lives are adequate when I
am preaching the deepest hope that is within me. I want to walk the
congregation out to the threshold of all I can see and invite them to leap
into the darkness of faith with me. I do not mean seducing them with
magical thinking about how they don't have to worry because everything is going to be rainbows and unicorns. I mean somehow having
the audacity to assert that we can trust in all of God's promises to us,
which are better than whatever unicorns we have dreamt up. Given the
scope of God's promises that I proclaim through my vision of the reign
of God, such preaching is inevitably daunting. The anxiety of making
such claims for God is probably why preachers are tempted to limit our
sermons to the safer topics of academic exegesis, congregational development, and moral exhortation. Those areas are all important components
of a sermon, but only as they provide a clarification or a response to the
vision of what God has promised for us. That core vision of what God
has promised and is delivering to us, proclaimed with passionate love for
God and our congregation, is what people come to church longing to
hear. It is also the good news with the power to transform lives.

Practical Preaching Choices

Our passion helps us make concrete decisions about what and how to
preach. The most important way our passion directs our preaching is

by reminding us only to preach what we really want to say. Neither the preacher nor the congregation needs to waste their time on something that does not stem from a passionate vision. In some cases that might mean I dig deeper within the scriptural text to find the connection to what I really want to say. Other times, I might pare a sermon down to the part that moves me and eliminate the rest. I would much rather cede part of my sermon time to the musicians to sing another inspirational hymn than to squander it by preaching sermonic filler. When I am praying for the sermon preparation and for my congregation, I usually find the right theme that I am excited to share with them.

Another way that passion informs our preaching is in connection to our long-term sermons. In chapter five, I talked about a variety of ways to choose a long-term sermon topic. As a preacher, an important part of that determination includes discerning where the congregation is poised to take another step toward our vision of the reign of God. For most of us, our hope for our congregations is more than we could expect to achieve in a lifetime, much less eighteen months. Deciding which element of that vision to focus on is congregational development work. However, we as preachers are going to have to have either a strong passion already or nurture our passion for the long-term sermon focus we select. Sustained preaching over such a period will be unbearable for us and for our listeners otherwise. Our passion to help our congregation get to the next stage of their congregational life is going to prod us and our church forward week by week.

Some preachers express their passion by condensing their vision of the reign of God into one short sentence. This sentence can be repeated regularly, almost as a personal mission statement. When leaders of congregations create a statement of their vision for themselves, their churches are led into their vision. Not every preacher does this, and only those with a strong passion for a particular aspect of their vision are likely to maintain it. Presiding Bishop Michael Curry proclaimed the Jesus Movement as a core statement of his vision of God's people, and then expanded his image to include *The Way of Love* as how the Jesus Movement is lived out. Bishop Sean Rowe in Northwestern Pennsylvania is known for his belief that "it's a great day in the Kingdom!" These and similar statements provide a way to distill a vision into an easy remembered nugget that can communicate and connect with others.

Finally, our passion can help us preach during those weeks when we are feeling overwhelmed. All preachers, but especially preachers who are the solo pastors of their parish, have weeks when everything seems to conspire against delivering a good sermon on Sunday morning. Whether we have difficult funerals, elaborate weddings, multiple unexpected pastoral visits, family celebrations or crises, a nasty flu bug, or any number of other matters filling up our calendar, finding the time to prepare and the energy to preach can be a struggle. During those weeks especially, we need a way to give a meaningful sermon that we can organize in whatever time we have available. Following our passion gives us two options.

The first option for preaching during a difficult week involves our current long-term sermon. We can preach the area of our greatest passion for the long-term sermon focus. We can talk to the congregation about where the extended sermon fits into our vision of the reign of God. We probably also have other aspects of what we have been preaching as part of that focus that we find particularly moving. Whether those elements are the theological rational, the practical vision for the future, or concrete ways the sermon focus is touching lives as it is lived out, by preaching those topics we will communicate our passion to the congregation without having to create a sermon from scratch. None of what we will say is likely to be new to us or the congregation, but reinforcing important points is part of the long-term sermon technique. On those rare occasions when I cannot prepare a sermon as usual, preaching those aspects of the long-term sermon that are most important to me still offers something worthwhile to the congregation.

A second option for preaching when we lack our usual preparation time is to give an account of the hope that is in us. We can, in effect, complete the sermon exercise that I shared at the beginning of this chapter. Unlike my time in seminary, however, today I can give that account, and hopefully all preachers can. My congregation always benefits when I express the vision of the reign of God arising out of my deepest hope. When I preach the core of that vision, my passion for helping my church share and live into that vision is going to be compelling. While I am preaching some aspect of that vision every week, I do not always preach the core of the vision. In a pinch, however, any of us can preach our vision of God's promise to us. Such a vision will probably take more than the three minutes I was originally given. Most congregations would gladly take three minutes, or thirty minutes, of passionate hope over a sermon that lacks it.

Questions for Reflection and Discussion

- What in this chapter motivated you to preach with passion?
- What preaching pitfalls are particularly tempting for you? How can tapping into your core passion and vision help you avoid them?
- Do you remember times that you have preached out of your passion and times that you have not? What was the difference?
- What was the scariest sermon for you to preach, or what was the most courageous sermon you have heard? What do you think provided the motivation for preaching such a strong sermon?
- What do you think would be different if preachers always preached with passion for their vision of the reign of God?

Practical Exercises

- Prepare a three-minute sermon on the hope that is within you.
- Make an appointment with someone who hears you preach regularly and ask them to describe what they understand your vision of the reign of God to be.

– 9 –

Personality

*So he appointed the twelve: Simon (to whom he gave the name
Peter); James son of Zebedee and John the brother of James (to
whom he gave the name Boanerges, that is, Sons of Thunder).*

—Mark 3:16–17

WHEN JESUS APPOINTED HIS twelve apostles, he knew he had some
strong personalities. Jesus called Simon Peter, who repeatedly spoke and
acted before he thought. Another Simon was known as either the Zealot
or the Cananaean (Luke 6:15, Mark 3:18). He also chose the sons of
Zebedee whom he called Sons of Thunder. They earned their nickname.
When a Samaritan village refused to receive Jesus and his companions,
James and John were ready to call down fire from heaven to destroy it
(Luke 9:51–55); I imagine there were other incidents that did not make
it into the Gospels.

Most commissions on ministry or parish call committees might
hesitate to move forward with a candidate whose resume prominently
displayed the nickname "Son of Thunder." Certainly, some follow-up
questions would be asked. Yet Jesus does not shy away from whatever

loud, thunderous, out-of-control qualities these two brothers exhibited. He chooses them as core members of the movement he was creating that would transform the world.

When Jesus chose James and John, we can assume he knew two things about them that are true for all those in ministry. First, their personalities could be an important asset in their work, and the epic scale of their ministries might require an animated and energetic character. Second, they were going to learn and grow, sanding off rough edges and acquiring skills and perspectives in ways that would benefit those they served. We notice that growth when John gets arrested with Peter in the fourth chapter of the Acts of the Apostles. His response is a now a proclamation of what he has seen and heard with no mention of even a desire to call down heavenly fire.

As preachers, our personalities are important components of what we bring to the pulpit. Like the Sons of Thunder, who we are allows us to communicate the gospel in a particular way. The ways we grow and change as the Holy Spirit works in and through us also provide avenues to proclaim the good news of Jesus's love and salvation.

Truth through Personality

Phillips Brooks, the rector of Trinity Church, Boston, and later bishop of Massachusetts, famously said, "Truth through personality is our description of real preaching."[1] In the Lyman Beecher Lectures in Preaching at Yale in 1877, Brooks spoke of the importance of the "individuality of every preacher" and how the God who sent each one to preach the gospel sent them "distinctly to preach it in [their] humanity."[2] Brooks reminded his hearers, "The truth you are preaching is the same" as that preached in the

---

1. Phillips Brooks, *Lectures on Preaching: Delivered Before the Divinity School of Yale College in January and February, 1877* (New York: E. P. Dutton and Company, 1888), 8.
2. Brooks, *Lectures on Preaching*, 23–24.

church across the street or on the other side of the world, but personality provides a "varying and growing element" that allows us to communicate that truth in an effective way to those in our particular congregation.[3]

Brooks said our personalities carry God's good news more powerfully as we deepen our faith and love. He was not looking for colorful personas filling the pulpit with gimmicks to transmit the gospel. He instructed his preachers, "Be yourself by all means, but let that good result come. . . . by winning a true self full of your own faith and your own love."[4] If we want to become people who can communicate the gospel, we must do the godly homework of living into the Great Commandment. "The real preparation of the preacher's personality for its transmissive work comes by the opening of [their] life on both sides, towards the truth of God and toward the needs of [humanity]."[5] As we expand our love of God and neighbor, we become more capable of sharing the good news of God's love in all the unique ways we have experienced it.

If our personality is a valuable asset in our preaching, then we need to bring it into the pulpit with us. We must find our own voice and be who we are. We draw from our own gifts and our own experiences to broadcast the timeless truth of the gospel in ways that can transform our congregation's lives today. Instead of trying to imitate other preachers, we have the commission to be fully who we are, but fully who we are given over to the service of proclaiming the gospel.

Living into our own personality in the pulpit can mean many different things, including not preaching from the pulpit at all. A notable example of someone who allowed their personality to carry their preaching is Romanos the Melodist. Legend has it that he was a lousy reader, but a great singer. After an encounter in his sleep with the Mother of God, he began to proclaim the Good News in song instead of speech.

---

3. Brooks, *Lectures on Preaching*, 28.
4. Brooks, *Lectures on Preaching*, 23.
5. Brooks, *Lectures on Preaching*, 26–27.

Some of his works still survive, although without his voice carrying them, they do not preach the same way they would have to his contemporaries.

Jesus's own personality came through in the ways that he preached. His use and choice of parables stems from the agricultural context of his native Nazareth. His stories included men and women and were sometimes open-ended. The way he describes the reign of God not only illuminates his subject, but also tells us about who Jesus is. Certainly, the Gospels are meant to provide us with an understanding of Jesus so that we can enter a deeper relationship with him. What we see are not only the objective attributes appropriate for the Son of God, but also the particular elements of Jesus's personality that proclaim the good news that the reign of God is at hand to the people of Nazareth, Samaria, and Galilee in the first century.

We can contrast the particulars of Jesus's personality with Paul's. Paul was a well-schooled rabbi and a Roman citizen. He seemed to prefer theological arguments to pastoral imagery. Many of his metaphors are drawn from sporting events and the legal system. Yet Paul's personality was able to reach multiple communities throughout the Mediterranean world, and his work still opens lives to God's good news today.

To use our own personalities to communicate the truth of the gospel effectively, we need to start with an awareness of who we are. We root ourselves in the particulars of where we are from, what we enjoy, and what our spiritual gifts are. Then we use who we are to share the good news that we know. God is much bigger than any single one of us, and we cannot hope to capture the entirety of the creator of the universe in one lifetime, much less one fifteen-minute sermon. Nor can we talk persuasively about those facets of God and God's life and work that we have not experienced. Instead, we start where we are, and if we preach the vision of the gospel that we can see from where we stand, our congregations will benefit.

Preaching the truth out of our personality does not mean that we get gimmicky. We do not need vestments matching our favorite football teams or open every sermon with an anecdote from the mystery novel we are reading that week. Drawing on our personality does mean, however, that we tap into our passions and are willing to speak in our native language of faith. I have one colleague whose faith is intensely rooted in the sacraments and ties almost all her sermons to either baptism or the Eucharist. I have another colleague who finds that the Hebrew Bible speaks powerfully to him, and so he preaches frequently on those texts. Preachers who are good storytellers should find ways to retell the biblical narratives in their own words. Musicians can include hymns in their sermons at the appropriate places. Those with office backgrounds can share how the Good News looks amid the craziness of the modern workplace. Travelers and missionaries bring experiences of the gospel expressed in different cultures. Preachers of different ages have different cultural contexts and use examples and illustrations drawn from different songs, books, and movies, and sometimes even from different media entirely.

Knowing who we are so we can draw upon those aspects of our personality in preaching is just the first step. We start by finding God where we are and sharing what we find. Then we heed Phillips Brooks's call to go deeper into our love for God and neighbor. How God transforms us with our own particular personality is a much more compelling witness to the gospel than who we are on our own.

Our Treasure in Clay Jars

Our strongest preaching springs from those places where we have experienced God's redemption and grace even in our weakness. Paul speaks to power of this kind of witness when he writes about how God's light shines "in our hearts to give the light of the knowledge of the glory of God in the face of Jesus Christ. But we have this treasure in clay jars, so that it may be made clear that this extraordinary power belongs to God" (2 Cor. 4:6–7). As preachers we want to share the incredible light that God has shone in our hearts, yet we proclaim that extraordinary power of God precisely when we feel weakest ourselves. Letting God's light shine through the areas of our own brokenness provides the clearest ways for people to see the strength of God who cares enough to act with healing and grace.

For most preachers, most of the time, this deepening of God's work in us is not a dramatic conversion story. Nor does preaching out of the places where God has ministered to us in our weakness mean that we are going into the pulpit to talk about our problems and how God has solved them every week. In the vast majority of cases, our church might not even be aware of the details of our experiences. The difference, however, is that we have been able to see God at work in a new and richer place in our lives. Our vision of the reign of God has expanded. We can share more, including perhaps what some in the congregation most need, because we have experienced God in the broken areas of our lives. As we are healed and delivered, we proclaim the good news about God that we did not know before. These are the sometimes small—yet always meaningful—steps of a life lived more and more fully with God.

We need to do our spiritual work to encounter God for ourselves. Our congregation also depends on us doing that work. If we do not grow, our church will suffer—especially if we are the senior pastor or a solo pastor. When we stay stuck, our church usually stays stuck with us. Preachers who have been preaching to the same congregation for many years shape their congregations. If the preacher has weaknesses or blind spots, the congregation will likely develop them too.

One of the worst ways for a preacher to try to push a congregation forward is to tell the church to do something that the preacher cannot or will not do. One aspect of preaching a long-term sermon is leading the congregation into where they are being called to go. A preacher cannot communicate the practical way forward if they have no experience of living into that change themselves. Nor can they preach a passionate vision of God acting in an area where they have never experienced God at work. Such lack of experience results in sermons begging people for money to pay the bills or to invite people to church because the Sunday school superintendent just retired.

Authors that look at leadership and change recognize the need for leaders to change themselves first. Edwin Friedman, whose teachings brought an understanding of family systems theory to many churches and synagogues, wrote that "before any technique or data could be effective, leaders had to be willing to face their own selves."[6] A leader cannot be taught to change a system until they look at the ways they are contributing to what needs to be changed.

Jesus made this point forcefully in Matthew 23 when he called the scribes and Pharisees "blind guides" and pointed out how damaging their own failings were to their congregation. He said, "Woe to you, scribes and Pharisees, hypocrites! For you cross sea and land to make a single convert, and you make the new convert twice as much a child of hell as yourselves" (Matt. 23:15).

Hopefully, we are not as blind or destructive to our churches as Jesus accused some of the religious leaders of being. Without a willingness to use the best spiritual and practical tools available to challenge ourselves, however, we ensure that any new converts we make are as broken as we are. Some of our work is nurturing our prayer life to draw closer to God and deepen our love for the congregation. Other aspects of our work include paying attention to wise people when they tell us what we don't want to hear. We need accountability to others in our own walks of discipleship if we hope our congregations might listen to us.

Preaching as We Grow

One of the reasons we explored different methods of determining a long-term sermon focus earlier is we, as preachers, have blind spots. I use the Natural Church Development survey to inform my long-term sermon focus because I need it. I have my favorite things to work on, and I also have areas that I tend not to see. I am much more likely to avoid matters

---

6. Edwin H. Friedman, *A Failure of Nerve: Leadership in the Age of the Quick Fix* (New York: Seabury Books, 1999), 21.

that I am not good at. Working with a wise coach, an outside consultant, or a solid process can point me in the right direction that I would otherwise miss.

Allowing God to work through aspects of our personality where we are weaker, as indicated by a church growth process, is not necessarily the stuff of epic theophanies. Often the growth is incremental and fairly straightforward. A recent long-term focus for our church and for my preaching was on loving relationships. A group of church members, who called themselves the Love Committee, identified ways we could improve the congregation's relationships with one another. Over the course of about two years I gave a long-term sermon on different aspects of loving relationships.

One of the areas identified was to be more intentional about thanking people and recognizing them for their work. A variety of mechanisms within the parish were developed and implemented to show our many hard-working volunteers greater appreciation for their efforts. Some of these ideas involved me directly and indirectly. We held a variety of recognition Sundays for various groups, where I called people up and thanked them during the liturgy and included something about them and their work in my sermon.

Beyond my concrete role in the committee's plans, I had to make other changes to be more appreciative and thankful in general. I had not been cold and heartless, and I often thanked people in person when I saw them. I also sent thank-you cards occasionally. Mostly, however, I was focused elsewhere, and did not look for ways to appreciate and acknowledge people in a consistent manner. My action, or inaction, made a difference. As the priest, I could recognize volunteers in sermons or announcements, or write cards to them, and they felt cherished and treasured by their church community as a result. I had been sliding by with a passing grade on appreciation, but for the church to live into the next stage of the life God was calling us to, I had to thank people at an A+ level.

I never preached about how I decided to be more appreciative of people. I just became more appreciative. Paying attention to that area, however, allowed me to talk about aspects of gratitude and thankfulness in my sermons in ways that I could not have before I lived into them.

In other cases, a preacher may decide to share what they are learning as they walk with the congregation in a new direction. A church that discerned a need to engage scripture more deeply may start a devotional Bible reading program. If the preacher recognizes that they have fallen into the rut of primarily reading scripture as preaching preparation, they could join the devotional program and preach about their insights.

Sometimes the congregation can benefit immensely by hearing the story of how we as preachers have overcome an issue that members of the congregation are struggling with. This sort of personal witness is a key staple in some preaching traditions. While rarer in the Episcopal Church and other mainline denominations, this style is present and can be effective. Such preaching can be especially powerful when the preacher has had to work through the issue the congregation is being asked to address in the current long-term sermon.

The most important point to keep in mind as preachers when we use ourselves as examples is that, to quote John the Baptist, Jesus "must increase, but I must decrease" (John 3:30). The goal of sharing how God has worked in an area of our weakness is to make clear how loving and powerful God is. The preacher is not the main character of the narrative; God is. We must talk about ourselves humbly and honestly, without trying to paint ourselves as either the worst sinner ever or the best saint. The more we resonate with the average congregation member in our struggles, the more likely people will be able to relate and learn from our example. Obviously, I am not talking about an evangelical conversion story here. That kind of witness has its own place. I am looking at issues where the preacher acts as the leader by scouting out a difficult path and then going back to help the congregation make the same journey.

I have given such a witness talk in the area of stewardship. I have not always had the healthiest relationship with money, and my wife and I made a few mistakes early in our marriage. At some point, though, we made the decision to tithe. The decision was not easy, but we stuck with it when things got tight. What we found was that God kept providing for us in ways we would never have imagined, and we were able to increase our giving as we prayed about our finances and asked God for help. Where I and my family am now is radically different from where we were fifteen years ago. Along the way, I have faced most of the struggles that my congregation encounters when dealing with questions of tithing and stewardship. By sharing my experience, I wanted to tell them that God will help them get through those difficulties if they push ahead. Since I rarely preach in this style, the few times I have done so have been effective.

Witness talks are a vivid way to express the truth through our developing personalities. Other less noticeable ways involve sharing practical tools or aspects of our vision with the congregation that we would not know except for the work we have done ourselves.

All Things to All People

Paul wrote to the Corinthians, "I have become all things to all people, that I might by all means save some" (1 Cor. 9:22b). Paul's personality did not change from sermon to sermon, but he recognized that his listeners had different backgrounds and needs, and that he had a responsibility to figure out how to communicate with all of them. We also know that not everyone in our congregations responds in the same way. Everyone has their own blend of experiences, preferences, and learning styles that cause us to respond to different people in different ways. Even though we will usually communicate most effectively out of a combination of our own strengths and experiences of God working in our weakness, our congregation will still benefit when we occasionally try something else. If we are the preacher the congregation hears almost all the time, mixing things up will be helpful for them, and maybe for us too.

I am not suggesting that we preach in ways that we cannot pull off. A tone-deaf preacher should not try to chant like Romonos, no matter how musical the congregation. Nor am I advocating using gimmicks or stunts that detract from the message instead of facilitating it. Using different approaches on occasion can help us continue to develop as preachers and offer a worthwhile variety to the congregation.

One way to offer a different approach is to change one element of our normal preaching. If we usually preach with a manuscript, we might sketch an outline. If we normally preach from the center, we could preach from a full manuscript in the pulpit. Some people react to the spontaneity of what seems to be just talking, while I find that reading a manuscript allows me to focus on crafting the text and then reading with more intentional emphases. Both styles are good but switching them up from time to time benefits both me and the congregation. If we preach on the gospel regularly, we might choose the psalm for a sermon. If our church has a stained-glass window or other artwork that corresponds to the scripture reading, we could walk to the window and talk about it.

Another way of expanding our preaching personality is to take advantage of the gifts that come from other people's personalities. Musicians can add music to the sermon. Congregants can act out a scripture reading or do a skit about the sermon theme. Artists can offer drawings or paintings that are published in the bulletin. One member of my congregation gave me a beautiful cross-stitch of numerous names for God. A few months later, for the Feast of the Holy Name, I took a picture of the cross-stitch, put it on the bulletin cover, and preached through the various names why each was important. Giving a children's sermon (or asking a gifted teacher to give one) is another way to mix things up to assist the proclamation of the gospel.

If we have questions about whether our preaching is reaching everyone, or if we need to try to expand our repertoire in some way, we can always ask. I specifically ask my vestry if they have any sermon feedback every couple of months. I have also given out sermon feedback forms on a couple of occasions to a select group of individuals. In cases where I have tried something that is significantly different than my normal style, I have told the congregation at the announcements that I am interested in any feedback they have. Usually a couple of people offer helpful comments.

Whatever we do, the important thing is that we are authentically doing it to share the gospel more effectively. If we are clear that our goal is to preach better, most congregations will appreciate and support the risks we take. More importantly, God will bless those risks as well.

Questions for Reflection and Discussion

- What surprised you in this chapter?
- What do you consider the strengths of your personality that you bring to your preaching?
- How have you had to grow in your own spiritual life or walk of discipleship in order to lead the congregation where they needed to go?
- How do you incorporate different styles into your sermons to reach people with different learning styles or experiences? What are two other ways that might be helpful for you to try in the future?

Practical Exercises

- Prepare a sermon based on how God showed up to help you in an area of your own weakness.
- Prepare a sermon that differs in some significant way from your normal preaching style.

− 10 −

Physicality

And the Word became flesh and lived among us.

—John 1:14a

WHEN THE WORD CAME down to sojourn on earth with us, that second person of the Trinity did not appear as a disembodied spirit. The Word became a full human being with a corporeal body. As one who became flesh, Jesus dealt with all blessings and challenges that physicality foists on preachers in their life and ministry.

While I was on a pilgrimage to the Holy Land, our guide took us by the Sea of Galilee. As most of us walked down the hill toward the shore of the lake, one person was held back and taken to a cave entrance high on the cliff face. When we were gathered at the bottom, our companion began to read the Beatitudes in a loud voice from above. Amazingly, all of us at quite a distance away could hear his proclamation clearly, even without microphones or electronic amplification. The physical landscape provided a natural augmentation to the sound. In Jesus's day, hundreds or even thousands of people could have heard someone preaching from that spot.

Jesus must have understood vocal projection and how sound travels in different environments. He took advantage not only of hillsides, but also went out into boats to exploit the way water surfaces carry sound. Nature would not have done all his work for him, though. He must also have taken deep breaths and maximized his sound production while keeping his balance as the fishing boat undulated upon the waves. Jesus not only had heavenly content but also mastered the physical aspects of sermon delivery so what he said could be clearly heard.

Consistently Excellent Preaching

This physical nature of preaching may be obvious to most people, but it was not to me. We all have our own gifts and our own blind spots. I had a much easier time exegeting scripture and coming up with a well-crafted sermon than I did consistently delivering it. I had done enough public speaking that I was comfortable in front of people, and often projected and communicated quite well. On a good day, everything went swimmingly. The problem was that some days just aren't good days.

A friend of mine who is a professional choreographer and dance instructor says that the difference between an amateur and a professional is not seen on the best days, but on the worst ones. Dedicated amateurs can sometimes rise to an exceedingly high level of performance. When things are not going well for an amateur, however, the quality level plummets. What makes a professional is their capacity to provide a consistently excellent product when they are tired, under the weather, underprepared, or when the performance space creates unexpected issues. Anyone with some luck or talent can have a high ceiling. Professionals have a high floor.

Preachers can all too easily assume that we are high caliber professionals based on our best days. On some Sunday mornings everything comes together and the Holy Spirit is clearly moving. We had something important to say that we were passionate about and that the congregation needed to hear. The sermon almost organized itself, and the right examples popped into our heads. The atmosphere was devoid of allergens and all the babies seemed to nap quietly at the most helpful time. On the way out the door, people who do not usually say anything mentioned a specific line that was meaningful to them, and at the Wednesday potluck, one table was discussing the sermon's implication for their ministry. With a few such weeks in a row, we can almost forget how challenging preaching can be.

Then we have an unexpected funeral or spend all day Saturday standing outside at our child's sporting event that goes into double overtime in a cold rain. None of the lectionary readings seem to click, a Sunday school teacher doesn't show up, and five minutes before the service no one can find the extra toilet paper. These are the weeks that tell us what kind of a preacher we are. A professional preacher still manages to provide a quality sermon that people can hear, that opens up the scriptures, and that has meaningful applications for the lives of individuals and the congregation. Maybe people realize that the preacher did not have their best week, but the people in the pews still go home with something from the sermon and no one is wishing it would just end.

On rough days, an amateur's sermon does not quite make it. Usually, the congregation understands. They wanted their priest to focus on the funeral and providing pastoral care to the deceased's family. They value the pastor supporting their children. They recognize everybody has off days. What we rarely hear from the congregation on those days, however, is what did not work and why. Those areas that prevent us from connecting on our worst days are the places we most need, and probably least want, to work on if we are going to improve as preachers.

If we can obtain adequate feedback, we might find that we spend all our time going down interesting exegetical rabbit holes but never come up with good applications that connect the scripture to Christians' everyday lives. We might skip over the scripture almost entirely if we have not had time to study it, opting instead for a running commentary on current events. Maybe we have all the pieces but unless we are focused, our points are so jumbled that the congregation spends all its time trying to figure out how things hang together. We might insert three "ums" into every sentence while we are thinking of what to say next. Or when slightly discombobulated, we might stop projecting so people miss large sections of what we said. Whatever our own Achilles's heel, we must deal with it to become the consistent preachers that our congregations—and those still outside of any congregation—need us to be.

I bring up this difference between amateur and professional preachers because we as preachers need to be willing to talk about how to become professionals. I have heard truly professional preachers on a bad day still give a sermon that shared the Good News in a way that made a difference to the congregation. I also know preachers who have preached sermons that were so powerful that I remember them a decade later, but whose next three sermons felt like checking a box between the gospel and the Nicene Creed. An especially dangerous time for many new preachers is when they preach a few amazing sermons, and then face the temptation to focus on other aspects of ministry because they feel that they have become "good preachers." Yet in every preaching survey I have seen, a higher percentage of preachers rate themselves as a "good preacher" than people in the pews rate their preacher as a "good preacher." We would all much rather focus on our successes but in preaching, as in most areas, we are only going to improve by attending to our difficulties.

Learning about Projection and Sound Production

My biggest difficulty was projection and sound production. I knew that sometimes I was louder than others, but I had two problems. The first was that I was not as loud as I thought I was, especially when I did not project well. The second was that I did not know how to make the necessary adjustments to get louder when I needed to. Overcoming these problems helped me learn a lot about aspects of physicality in preaching.

Eighteen months into my second parish call, during a mutual ministry review process, one of my lay leaders asked to talk to me. He said that the questions others asked got him thinking about my preaching and that he did not want to give feedback without thinking it through and talking directly to me. What he noticed, as he paid attention to my preaching, was that I had a habit of getting softer at the end of my sentences. They would trail off. That single bad habit, which I was completely unaware of, had created a barrier for people who were listening.

His comments sent me scurrying to correct what I was doing. A few other trusted listeners confirmed that he had identified a real issue, although they had not isolated it themselves. I found someone who helped me think about speaking through the end of sentences. One suggestion was to imagine saying, "Amen," after each sentence so I finished them well. I also wrote out full manuscript sermons for a while. If I was not thinking about what I was going to say, I could focus on how I said it. By preparing and practicing, I created a slightly different intonation pattern that didn't fall off the table as a sentence ended. This work did not eliminate the tendency. In conversations, I can still find my sentences trailing off. Attending to this issue has allowed me to minimize this inclination when I preach, however, which means the congregation hears what I am saying most of the time. My unhelpful habit does not interfere now with the delivery of my message.

My other physical issue was that I could not project more when I realized I was speaking too softly. I just did not know how. I eventually discovered the issue was my breathing and posture; when those basic aspects of sound production are not aligned, trying to be louder is counterproductive. At the time, all I knew was if I was nervous or had bad allergies, I would often open my mouth and not be as loud as I wanted to be. I did not know how things would sound before I spoke, and if I didn't like what I heard I was stuck.

What helped me finally overcome this issue was a three-day acting class using the Alexander technique. According to its website, the

Alexander technique helps "identify and lose the harmful habits you have built up over a lifetime of stress and learn to move more freely."[1] Applied to acting, this technique focuses on "the relationship of the coordination of the muscles, sensory appreciation . . . and thinking. If an actor is performing with rigidity . . . [b]oth the actor and the audience will typically experience this as poor vocal production, lack of freedom in movement and tense expression of emotions."[2] Preachers are similar to actors in their need to be present to what they are saying and to allow their whole body to help express their message. When we are unaware of what our bodies are doing when we are speaking, or even how they work to produce sound, we get in our own way. Having a few days of focused work on integrating our physical being with a text can advance our preaching technique.

What I discovered was that I often held stress in my body in ways that interfered with my ability to speak loudly and clearly. Specifically, I often scrunched my shoulders, and if I was standing in front of a congregation and got nervous, I locked my knees. After a bit of work, I learned to bend my knees and drop my shoulders as I prepared to speak. I also experienced what it felt like to speak freely compared to being constrained and how to go back and forth from one sensation to the other. Being able to recognize when I was not projecting well, and having the tools to correct it, was a huge blessing for me and for my congregation.

Focusing on my posture generally made a difference. I was never involved in an activity growing up that forced me to maintain good posture, so I developed bad habits. Bad posture meant, among other things, I did not breathe well or have optimal breath control. For me, taking adult dance classes helped me to pay attention to my posture and breathe properly. Yoga is another discipline that can help preachers pay

---

1. "The Complete Guide to the Alexander Technique," accessed May 17, 2019, https://www.alexandertechnique.com/.
2. Tom Vasiliades, "The Alexander Technique: An Acting Approach," accessed May 17, 2019, https://www.alexandertechnique.com/articles/acting3/.

attention to our breath and recognize what is happening with our bodies as we work.

Visualizing and Pacing What We Say

The Alexander technique acting class also taught me to create an image in my mind of the words I am saying. When I have a visual of what I am describing as I speak, the way I speak changes. I emphasize different words. My rhythm is usually different than if I am not picturing what I am saying. Much good preaching involves helping people draw mental pictures. When we retell a scripture story, we fill in some gaps to help people imagine the setting, or even to imagine themselves in the setting. What I found, however, was that I could do the imaging work as part of my preparation. During the sermon, sometimes I focused on relating the description, but not on reimaging the scene again in my mind. When I visualized what I was saying as I preached, the excitement came through in my voice, my expressions, and my gestures in more engaging ways. The acting work helped me focus on visualizing what I wanted to talk about.

Besides filling out our investment in the what we are saying, imagining and visualizing can also slow down our speech pattern. Slowing down is important because we can read a text out loud faster than people can understand it. Teresa L. Fry Brown in *Delivering the Sermon* notes that "[a]n average reading rate is 135 to 175 words per minute; often preachers use this as his or her speaking rate. The preacher must consider the hearing patterns of the listener."[3] This reading rate is faster than we speak in normal conversations. A manuscript preacher can get into trouble reading through a text at a clip beyond the congregation's comprehension speed. Even when preaching through something we have prepared but not written out, our pace can be much faster than we would talk in conversation. Slowing down and using our extra time to

3. Teresa L. Fry Brown, *Delivering the Sermon: Voice, Body, and Animation in Proclamation* (Minneapolis, MN: Fortress Press, 2008), 40.

emphasize what we are saying by varying our tone, pitch, and rhythm enriches our preaching.

The temptation to read through texts too quickly is, I think, the reason many congregations say they prefer preachers who are not using manuscripts. Over the years, I have heard numerous comments from listeners who prefer to have preachers "just talk" to them. The real problem, however, is not the manuscript, but how the manuscript is read. The advantage of a manuscript is the ability to craft a sermon with compelling imagery, balance, and poetry. Since the words are prepared, the preacher can focus on properly enacting text in the moment. When we read without regard for the limitations inherent in speaking and listening, preachers undermine what should be a strength of the manuscript style. I do not believe preaching with a manuscript is better or worse than not using one. Whatever we do, however, we have a responsibility to do it well.

Gestures and Movement

Visualizing what we are talking about while we preach can also aid our gestures and movement. When I am imagining what I am saying, I can put myself in a special relationship with the action and bring the congregation along with me. I have found my gestures are more natural, and seem to be more comprehensible, when my hands and even my body are pointing or turning based on narrative I am describing. If I take a step somewhere, I am not just walking around, but I am moving toward or away from something I am talking about.

To give an example, if the Bible passage I am preaching on has Jesus debating with a group of religious leaders, I think about them standing in front of me. I can see Jesus standing on my left and his interlocutors on my right. I slightly turn toward where Jesus is or gesture in that direction when I talk about him. I focus in the other direction when his opponents speak. I can keep those simple gestures going throughout a sermon without having to think about whether I am motioning in the right direction because I picture them standing there. Even if I move to other points in the sermon for a while and come back the Bible passage, I will know where Jesus is standing and remain consistent in my gestures.

The same holds true for the application aspects of a sermon. If I am talking about the congregation's life, I want to see people going out the front doors to welcome people, or going downstairs to the food pantry, or upstairs to the children's Sunday school classes. If I envision people doing what the gospel is calling us to do, my gestures and motions will indicate what I see. Since the people in the pews know where the front doors are and where different ministries are located, they are going to grasp what I am doing as well. The clearer the image is in my mind, the clearer I can communicate that image to the congregation. If I do not take the time to visualize my sermon, however, it will be much harder to connect my gestures and movement to the message.

Caring for Our Preaching Instrument

All performers need to ensure they maintain their instrument. Whether we are tuning a piano, changing reeds and guitar strings, or ensuring a proper humidity level for our cello, those who create sound for a living know what they need to address. As preachers, we are our instrument, and how we care for ourselves matters. Brown's *Delivering the Sermon* contains a variety of helpful information about aspects of physicality in preaching. She also includes valuable exercises to help a preacher improve in areas of weakness. She discusses a variety of breathing problems and causes of vocal fatigue that can plague preachers.[4] These issues, and almost any others in our preaching, can be due to either physical or emotional difficulties, or a combination of both. One issue Brown does not shy away from is the danger of trying to preach in a voice that is not authentic. For some preachers, our natural voice does not sound like the ideal preacher's voice we have in our head. Comments from congregants

---

4. Brown, *Delivering the Sermon*, 30–31.

may reinforce this disconnect. Trying to preach like somebody else is both a vocational and physical issue, however. Brown says, "When the preacher is comfortable and assured that God has given both the call and authority one can speak in one's voice and stop masquerading. The vocal structure may not be able to sustain a style or voice heard in someone else."[5] Until we are comfortable with how the word comes into our own flesh, we are not going to be physically able to be the preacher we were called to be.

Brown suggests that preachers get annual hearing exams, so that we know what we sound like and can monitor the response of listeners as well.[6] This commonsense suggestion is not one I had previously heard. All preachers would benefit from making sure that all the physical pieces of our vocal mechanism and our hearing are in good working order.

Taking care of one's voice in the midst of all the Sunday morning requirements is both important and not easy. Especially when priests and pastors preside over a liturgy and preach, sometimes more than once on a Sunday, Brown's advice echoes many others' in suggesting quiet and vocal rest to the degree feasible Sunday morning or trying to avoid talking on Monday.[7] I have also found a number of other techniques that help me get through a full Sunday morning when vocal rest is hard to come by.

One practice I have found important is to stay as hydrated as possible on Saturday. While being hydrated on Sunday is good, I often cannot drink enough water or other fluids in time to get my voice well lubricated before my morning services. Drinking nonalcoholic liquid all day Saturday can be effective, though, as is avoiding things that are going to dehydrate me.

---

5. Brown, *Delivering the Sermon*, 33.
6. Brown, *Delivering the Sermon*, 35.
7. Brown, *Delivering the Sermon*, 34.

On the way to church Sunday morning, I do vocal warmup exercises in my car. I have a series of scales, along with some tongue twisters. Part of expressive preaching involves avoiding preaching in a monotone. The more warmed up my voice is, the better my range and the more I can get out of it. I have also discovered the hard way that one of the quickest ways to mess up my voice for the day is to get excited about the opening hymn and sing loudly while my voice is still cold. If I have time to step into the choir room when our musicians are warming up, I try to do that as well.

I live in a part of the country with lots of allergens, and my church loves to see the sacristy bursting with flowers. Some mornings, my eyes love the floral beauty but my sinuses disagree. Besides paying extra attention to posture, hydration, and other issues, I have found small facial massages to be extremely helpful those mornings. Just taking my thumb and forefinger and pushing hard around my eye socket, down the top of my nose, and around my mouth can open needed sinus space for me to be able to speak freely and clearly. Spending two minutes before every service rubbing my face would be a good idea, but when I have to speak with a stuffy head this practice is unavoidable.

Before I was ordained, I probably would not have believed how crucial an effect physicality has on preaching. I had heard of the preacher's nap but did not realize how physically taxing good preaching can be, especially when combined with other Sunday morning responsibilities. Between the engagement of core muscles for breath support, standing for long periods, and making gestures large enough to be seen from the back pew, the preacher gets a workout. I have had busy Sundays when the only times I sat down from 7:00 am until noon was during the scripture readings. At the same time, when I preach, I want to give it everything I have. I hope I go home exhausted because I have poured every ounce of energy and enthusiasm I can muster into sharing the gospel with my congregation. To maintain a high level of energy for preaching means paying attention to the many physical aspects of preaching discussed in this chapter. I cannot do my job if I focus on the message and ignore my instrument.

Questions for Reflection and Discussion

- What in this chapter made you think about preaching with physicality differently?
- What areas of preaching are your strongest and what areas do you need to work on to become a consistent preaching professional?
- How do you think about physical elements of your sermon such as pacing, vocal pitch and tone, gestures, and movement in preparation for preaching?
- How do you care for your preaching instrument?

Practical Exercises

- Prepare a three-minute sermon that you give without speaking, but only using gestures and expressions.
- Ask three lay leaders to spend a month paying attention to the pacing, pitch and tone of your voice, your facial expressions, and your gestures and movements, and to provide constructive feedback.

Conclusion

PREACHING IS PARADOXICAL. Our best preaching is an offering created at the core of our spiritual and emotional lives, and we share it freely and openly for the benefit of our congregations. It requires of us both audacity and humility. It evokes responses ranging from exhilaration to terror in the preacher, and from inspiration to boredom in the listener. Our upcoming Sunday sermon constantly hovers at the back of our consciousness as we go through the week, while our time to focus on it gets repeatedly delayed by the day's distractions. Few aspects of our ministry have as much impact as our preaching and getting helpful feedback on improving it is exceedingly difficult.

One of our challenges as preachers is that most of our colleagues are busy preaching when we are. On the occasions we hear each other preach, the context is often a funeral or some special service. As a solo pastor leading worship almost every week, I rarely hear others preaching to their congregations on a Sunday morning. I have few opportunities to learn from them or to talk about their sermons. Their duties prevent them from showing up in my church as well.

Improving our craft requires significant vulnerability. We may need to ask for specific feedback from insightful parishioners who care enough to tell us the truth. We may need to ask experienced colleagues to take time out of their busy schedules to hear a sermon and tell us what they think. We almost certainly need to admit to ourselves that we could be better preachers than we are, and then do the work to figure out how we might improve.

We also face a rapidly changing preaching environment. Our churches require leadership—including leadership in their pulpits—that few have been prepared for. Increasing numbers of unchurched and de-churched people need to hear the gospel message. Fifty years ago, a congregation might have been able to survive a season of mediocre preaching in exchange for good pastoral care or administrative competency. Today, churches cannot afford such bargains. If our preaching does not transform our congregation, we need to change our approach until it does.

This book is an invitation to think together about our calling to preach. In a challenging environment, I have had to conceive of my preaching task in new ways while continuing to develop my basic preaching skills. I have learned, often the hard way, how to lead a congregation into a new stage of development while grounding my proclamation in my own passion and vision. I have been blessed with feedback, including feedback I did not want at the time, that helped me preach more effectively. I have also had the blessing of colleagues that I could ask for help and advice along the way.

You have probably faced similar challenges and found your own ways to answer them. I hope this book will help you with elements of your preaching and prompt you to share your insights with colleagues. The more we as preachers make time to work together and strengthen one another, the more we and our churches will benefit. I also hope that we find ways to invite our congregations into our preaching process. Any sermon, but especially a long-term sermon, is much richer when we utilize the gifts and wisdom of our entire congregation. The more we approach our calling as a community commission instead of an individual assignment, the more likely our preaching will truly transform our congregations.

Appendix

A Curriculum for a Long-Term Sermon Preaching Course

THIS BOOK CAN BE USED as the basis for a homiletics course that develops basic preaching skills while also developing competencies in transformational congregational leadership. Such a course would be especially appropriate for a doctor of ministry course or a local formation course, but could also be done in a colleague group dedicated to preaching development. What follows is a basic curriculum using this book that could be adapted to a variety of different contexts.

Curriculum Goals

This curriculum will help students achieve the following:

- Improvement in overall preaching.
- Understanding a long-term sermon.
- Experience in choosing a long-term sermon goal appropriate for a congregation.
- Understanding of the components of preaching a long-term sermon and how to incorporate them into weekly sermons.
- Understanding of and improvement in preaching with prayer, passion, personality, and physicality.

Curriculum Arrangement

This curriculum is broken up into ten sections, each section corresponding to one book chapter. Depending on the course structure and number of participants, these sections could be covered in a single session or multiple shorter sessions. Each section includes time for peer preaching review, as well as discussion questions and exercises to develop an understanding of skills from the relevant chapter. For some sections, the sermon for peer review will be a general sermon chosen by the preacher. In other sections, the sermon will be part of an exercise specifically relevant to the topic being discussed. If a curricular section is broken up into multiple class sessions, each session will ideally include one or more sermon presentations and some element of topical discussion. Such a setup recognizes that preachers will be more focused on a general discussion after they have preached, and the fewer preachers on any given day, the more energy the group overall is likely to have for other work.

Peer Preaching Review

One of the best ways to develop general preaching skills is to preach and receive solid feedback. Ideally every participant would preach a peer-reviewed sermon during each section. If class size and timing prevent that volume of preaching, a rotation where everyone preaches at least one general sermon of their choosing along with chapter specific sermon exercises should be designed. These sermons should approximate as closely as possible the sermons being preached in the preacher's current context. This means that sermon length and style, except where otherwise specified, as well as the preacher's dress and other sermon elements, can vary between students.

During and after each sermon, the preacher's peers fill out a sermon evaluation sheet and share the results following a discussion of the sermon. If possible, the sermons should be recorded so the preacher can review the sermon video in light of the comments received.

The following questions can be used for a sermon evaluation sheet.

- What did you hear in the sermon?
- What did you think the main point of sermon was?
- Provide a basic outline of the sermon.
- What specifically was said that helped you connect with the sermon?
- What specifically was said that did not help you connect with the sermon?
- What other preaching features, such as the preacher's tone of voice, pitch, volume, pacing, enunciation, gestures, movement, or handouts, were helpful?
- What other preaching features, such as the preacher's tone of voice, pitch, volume, pacing, enunciation, gestures, movement, or handouts, were not helpful?
- What other comments do you have for the preacher?

Assignments, Discussion Questions, and Class Presentations for Each Section

Section One

Assignments

- Read the introduction and chapter one.
- Prepare a sermon to present.
- Ask your vestry or parish board what themes they think are most important for you to preach about in the coming weeks.

Discussion Questions

- What in this chapter made you think about preaching in a different way?
- When in your ministry have you stopped sharing a vision that was needed for change too quickly?

- What is the longest you have ever maintained a preaching focus?
- In what ways does the analogy of preaching as learning a new language resonate with you? In what ways is it challenging?
- What experiences have you had of coordinating sermons with other preachers or of getting input about sermon themes from congregants?

Class Presentations

- Share the results of your conversation with your vestry or parish board. Pick one theme they identified and show how you could insert something about that theme into the sermon you preached for this section.

Section Two

Assignments

- Read chapter two.
- Prepare a sermon to present.
- Think about a change you would like to see in your congregation. Write a five-hundred-word outline of a condensed practical vision of how things would be different if the change were made, the theological rationale for why God is calling the congregation to a new place, and the practical skills the congregation needs in order to move forward.

Discussion Questions

- What aspects of the extended stewardship sermon discussion struck you? Did any of the choices make you uncomfortable?
- What do you see as the advantages and disadvantages of breaking traditional homiletical guidelines in favor of incorporating long-term sermon material?

- Are there particular times you think congregations need to hear practical visions of the future, theological rationales for change, or instructions for developing specific skills and practices?
- What are the strengths and weaknesses of lectionary preaching? How might those weaknesses be ameliorated through an extended sermon focus?
- Think about a time you have preached on something besides the scripture passages appointed for the day. What motivated your choice? What fruit came from that choice?
- Did any of the sermons described in this section make assumptions about the congregation's understanding or capacity that may not have been accurate?

Class Presentations

- Share your paper on elements necessary for preaching toward a change you would like to see in your congregation.

Section Three

Assignments

- Read chapter three.
- Prepare a sermon to present.
- Write a five-hundred-word summary of the practical effects a positive change in your congregation would have. Describe the current problems and paint a picture of the church with those problems transformed into opportunities and blessings.
- Pick three teachings or parables of Jesus that function as practical visions that motivate people to change.

Discussion Questions

- How did this chapter add to you thinking about how to motivate a congregation toward change?
- How has a preacher offering a theological rationale motivated you to change in the past?
- What ways do you generally offer a practical vision? Do you favor drawing a picture of the future, describing current problems in the church, or looking at the wider community? Do you find different aspects more helpful with different themes? Can you describe a time you put all the elements together?
- When has a congregation been motivated to make a change by your preaching? What elements were most important in inspiring that action?
- What parables and teachings of Jesus function as practical visions that motivate people to change?

Class Presentations

- Share your essay on the effects a positive change in your congregation would have.

Section Four

Assignments

- Read chapter four.
- Prepare a sermon to present.
- Develop a five-hundred-word outline of a sermon series on a topic of your choice. The outline should include relevant scripture passages, sermon points, practical exercises, and descriptions of handouts.

Discussion Questions

- What subject in this chapter was most helpful in thinking about your own preaching?
- What practical skills, if any, have you taught during a sermon?
- Can you identify areas where a lack of understanding of how to engage in particular discipleship practices is preventing your congregation from moving forward?
- How might your congregation be different if congregational activity was frequently highlighted in preaching and parishioners were asked to participate in the sermon?
- What parishioner gifts could you regularly include in your preaching?

Class Presentations

- Share your sermon series outline.

Section Five

Assignments

- Read chapter five.
- Prepare a sermon to present.
- Write a sentence describing what you think your congregation's current minimum factor is. Share that sentence with your board or other key leaders and get their feedback.
- Research one of the processes suggested for discerning a long-term sermon focus. Coordinate with your classmates to ensure all four processes are covered. Prepare a short summary of what you learned.

Discussion Questions

- What in this chapter made you think differently about how to determine a focus for your preaching?
- Does thinking about a series of long-term sermons as a succession of interim efforts to move a congregation make the idea more or less appealing to you? Why?
- What processes have you used in the past to discern a congregational development or long-term sermon focus?
- What kind of discernment process do you think would be most helpful for you to identify an appropriate focus for your congregation at this time?
- Some preachers have advocated preaching with the Bible in one hand and a newspaper in the other. Compare and contrast that approach with one that pays particular attention to congregational survey results as well.
- Have you ever preached or heard sermons on a congregation's mission statement? What seemed to work and what didn't in those sermons?

Class Presentations

- Share your assessment of your congregation's minimum factor, and the response of your congregational leaders.
- Share your findings about one of the processes that can aid in determining a long-term sermon focus.

Section Six

Assignments

- Read chapter six.
- Prepare a sermon to present.

■ Create a detailed eight- to twelve-page outline for a long-term sermon series on spiritual gifts, *The Way of Love*, or another topic appropriate to your congregation. What is the theological rationale, practical vision, and concrete skills that need to be taught? Include a timeline, scripture readings to use, congregational examples, parishioner gifts to incorporate, and handouts to distribute.

Discussion Questions

■ What did you learn in this chapter that helped you better understand a long-term sermon?

■ How do the two extended sermon models differ from other work you have experienced around spiritual gifts or *The Way of Love*? What do you think the difference in results would be?

■ What most excites you about maintaining a consistent sermon theme over an extended period? What most scares you?

■ What techniques described in this or earlier chapters would be the biggest departures from your normal preaching style?

Class Presentations

■ Share your long-term sermon outline.

Section Seven

Assignments

■ Read chapter seven.
■ Prepare a sermon to present.
■ Spend a week engaging in some of the prayer practices described in this chapter that are not part of your normal routine in preparation for preaching. After the sermon, summarize in five hundred

words how the prayer felt and what difference, if any, you experienced as part of the sermon and the surrounding worship.

■ Make a list of emphases you would like prayed for as you prepare your preaching. Share that list with the leaders in your congregation and ask them to take responsibility for praying along with you.

Discussion Questions

■ What elements of this chapter made you think about the connection between prayer and preaching in a new way?

■ Of the kinds of prayer described in this chapter, which ones feel most important for preaching to bear fruit?

■ What have been your customary prayer practices in preparation for preaching? What new prayer disciplines are you interested in beginning?

■ What role do you think the prayers of the congregation have on preaching? How might the congregation be invited to take that role more seriously?

Class Presentations

■ Share your reflections on praying in preparation for preaching.

■ Share the prayer emphases you choose, and what happened as they were shared with the congregation.

Section Eight

Assignments

■ Read chapter eight.
■ Prepare a sermon to present.
■ Prepare a three-minute sermon on the hope that is within you.

- Make an appointment with someone who hears you preach regularly and ask them to describe what they understand your vision of the reign of God to be.

Discussion Questions

- What in this chapter motivated you to preach with passion?
- What preaching pitfalls are particularly tempting for you? How can tapping into your core passion and vision help you avoid them?
- Do you remember times that you have preached out of your passion and times that you have not? What was the difference?
- What was the scariest sermon for you to preach, or what was the most courageous sermon you have heard? What do you think provided the motivation for preaching such a strong sermon?
- What do you think would be different if preachers always preached with passion for their vision of the reign of God?

Class Presentations

- Preach your sermon on the hope that is within you.
- Share the feedback you received about how your vision of the reign of God is understood, and how that might differ from your understanding of what you are preaching.

Section Nine

Assignments

- Read chapter nine.
- Prepare a sermon based on how God showed up to help you in an area of your own weakness.

Discussion Questions

- What surprised you in this chapter?
- What do you consider the strengths of your personality that you bring to your preaching?
- How have you had to grow in your own spiritual life or walk of discipleship in order to lead the congregation where they needed to go?
- How do you incorporate different styles into your sermons to reach people with different learning styles or experiences? What are two other ways that might be helpful for you to try in the future?

Class Presentations

- Share what it felt like to prepare, preach, and receive feedback about a sermon on how God showed up to help you in an area of your own weakness. Share other experiences you have had of preaching on similar themes.

Section Ten

Assignments

- Read chapter ten.
- Prepare a sermon that differs in some significant way from your normal preaching style.
- Prepare a three-minute sermon that you give without speaking, but only using gestures and expressions.
- Ask a leader in your congregation to provide constructive feedback about your pacing, the pitch and tone of your voice, your facial expressions, and your gestures and movements.

Discussion Questions

- What in this chapter made you think about preaching with physicality differently?
- What areas of preaching are your strongest and what areas do you need to work on to become a consistent preaching professional?
- How do you think about physical elements of your sermon such as pacing, vocal pitch and tone, gestures, and movement in preparation for preaching?
- How do you care for your preaching instrument?

Class Presentations

- Preach your sermon using only gestures and expressions.
- Share your feedback from a congregational leader on the pacing, the pitch and tone of your voice, your facial expressions, and your gestures and movements. Note how this is similar or different from feedback you have received from your preaching peers.

Final Assignment

Write a ten- to fifteen-page paper describing key learnings from this course and how you will incorporate them into your preaching. This paper can include elements of a long-term sermon to be preached, sermon outlines, or personal habits to improve preaching with prayer, passion, personality, or physicality. Ideally, this paper will outline practical next steps to aid future preaching that transforms your congregation.